Catherine of Aragon

Catherine of Aragon

An Illustrated History

Carol-Ann Johnston

First published in Great Britain in 2025 by
Pen & Sword History
An imprint of Pen & Sword Books Limited
Yorkshire – Philadelphia

Copyright © Carol-Ann Johnston 2025

ISBN 978 1 03611 110 6

The right of Carol-Ann Johnston to be identified as
Author of this Work has been asserted by her in accordance
with the Copyright, Designs and Patents Act 1988.

A CIP catalogue record for this book is
available from the British Library.

All rights reserved. No part of this book may be reproduced, transmitted, downloaded, decompiled or reverse engineered in any form or by any means, electronic or mechanical including photocopying, recording or by any information storage and retrieval system, without permission from the Publisher in writing. NO AI TRAINING: Without in any way limiting the Author's and Publisher's exclusive rights under copyright, any use of this publication to 'train' generative artificial intelligence (AI) technologies to generate text is expressly prohibited. The Author and Publisher reserve all rights to license uses of this work for generative AI training and development of machine learning language models.

Typeset by Mac Style
Printed in the UK by CPI Group (UK) Ltd, Croydon, CR0 4YY.

The Publisher's authorised representative in the EU for product safety is Authorised Rep Compliance Ltd., Ground Floor, 71 Lower Baggot Street, Dublin D02 P593, Ireland.
www.arccompliance.com

For a complete list of Pen & Sword titles please contact

PEN & SWORD BOOKS LIMITED
47 Church Street, Barnsley, South Yorkshire, S70 2AS, England
E-mail: enquiries@pen-and-sword.co.uk
Website: www.pen-and-sword.co.uk
or
PEN AND SWORD BOOKS
1950 Lawrence Road, Havertown, PA 19083, USA
E-mail: uspen-and-sword@casematepublishers.com
Website: www.penandswordbooks.com

In loving memory of my Nana Irene, who did not see this work finished.

Contents

Acknowledgements		viii
Preface		xiii
Chapter 1	Infanta of Spain	1
Chapter 2	Princess of Wales	12
Chapter 3	Uncertain Times	29
Chapter 4	Queen of England	45
Chapter 5	Good Queen Catherine	55
Chapter 6	Motherhood	82
Chapter 7	Anne Boleyn and The King's Great Matter	91
Chapter 8	Exile	114
Chapter 9	Death of the Queen	136
Chapter 10	Afterlife	145
Appendices		159
Appendix 1: A Comprehensive List of Preparations for Catherine's Funeral		160
Appendix 2: Will of Katharine of Arragon		162
Appendix 3: Detailed Report of Catherine of Aragon's Funeral		163
Appendix 4: Excerpt from a Letter Written by Jean De Ponte to Thomas Cromwell Regarding the Tapers at Catherines Tomb		167
Appendix 5: Excerpt from the Last Will and Testament of Queen Mary I Regarding her Desire to be Laid to Rest Alongside her Mother		168
Notes		169
Bibliography		175
Index		176

Acknowledgements

I am indebted to Sarah-Beth Watkins for offering me this chance and for her help and support throughout writing this book and to Sarah Hodder for her patience and help throughout the editing process and for all our little chats that I thoroughly enjoyed.

I would also like to thank Amy McElroy for providing the family trees so helpful to tracking the various members of Catherine's family and the Tudor dynasty.

Finally, to all my family and friends who offered advice and critique of *Jane Seymour: An Illustrated Life*, you have no idea what your support has meant, thank you.

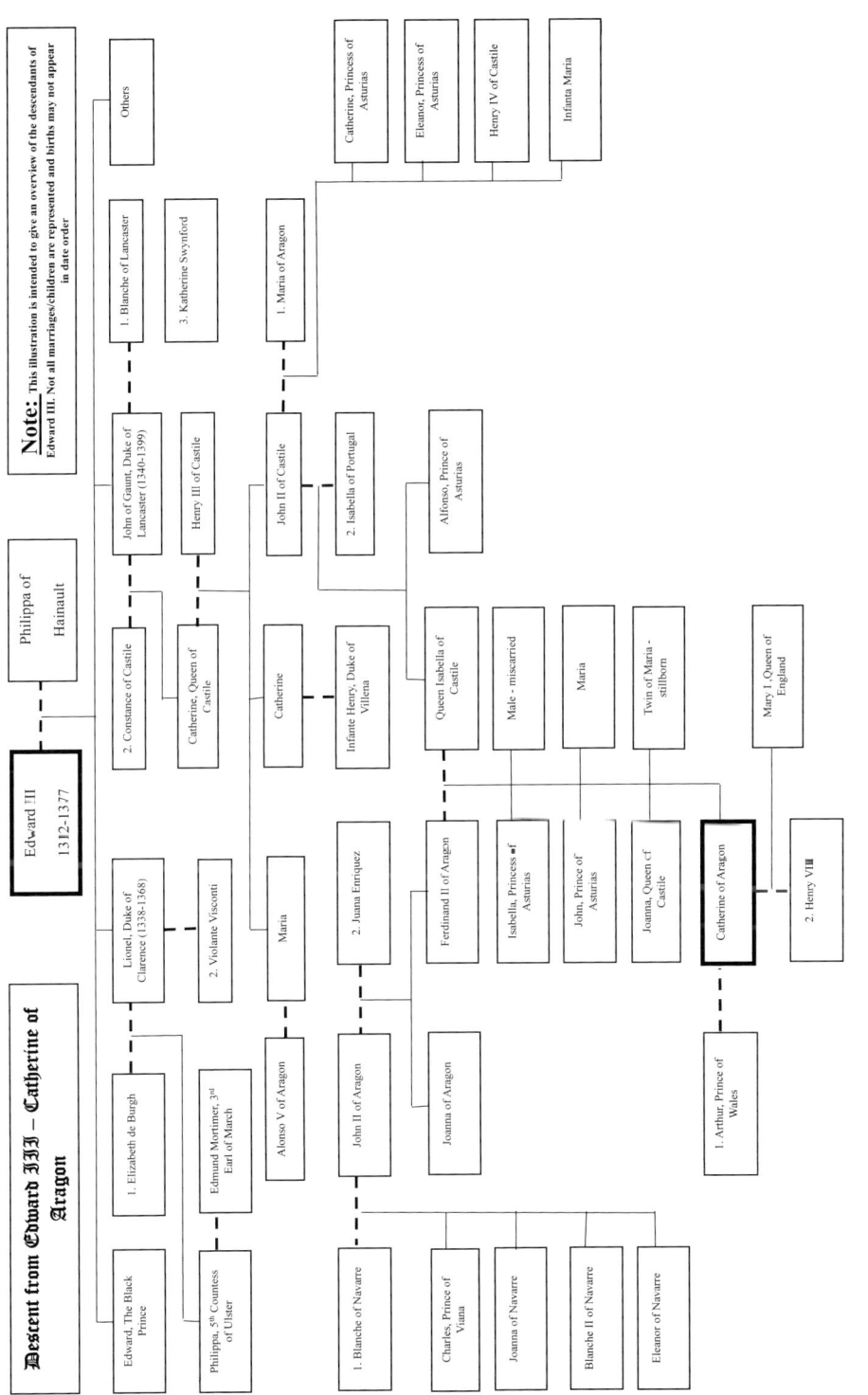

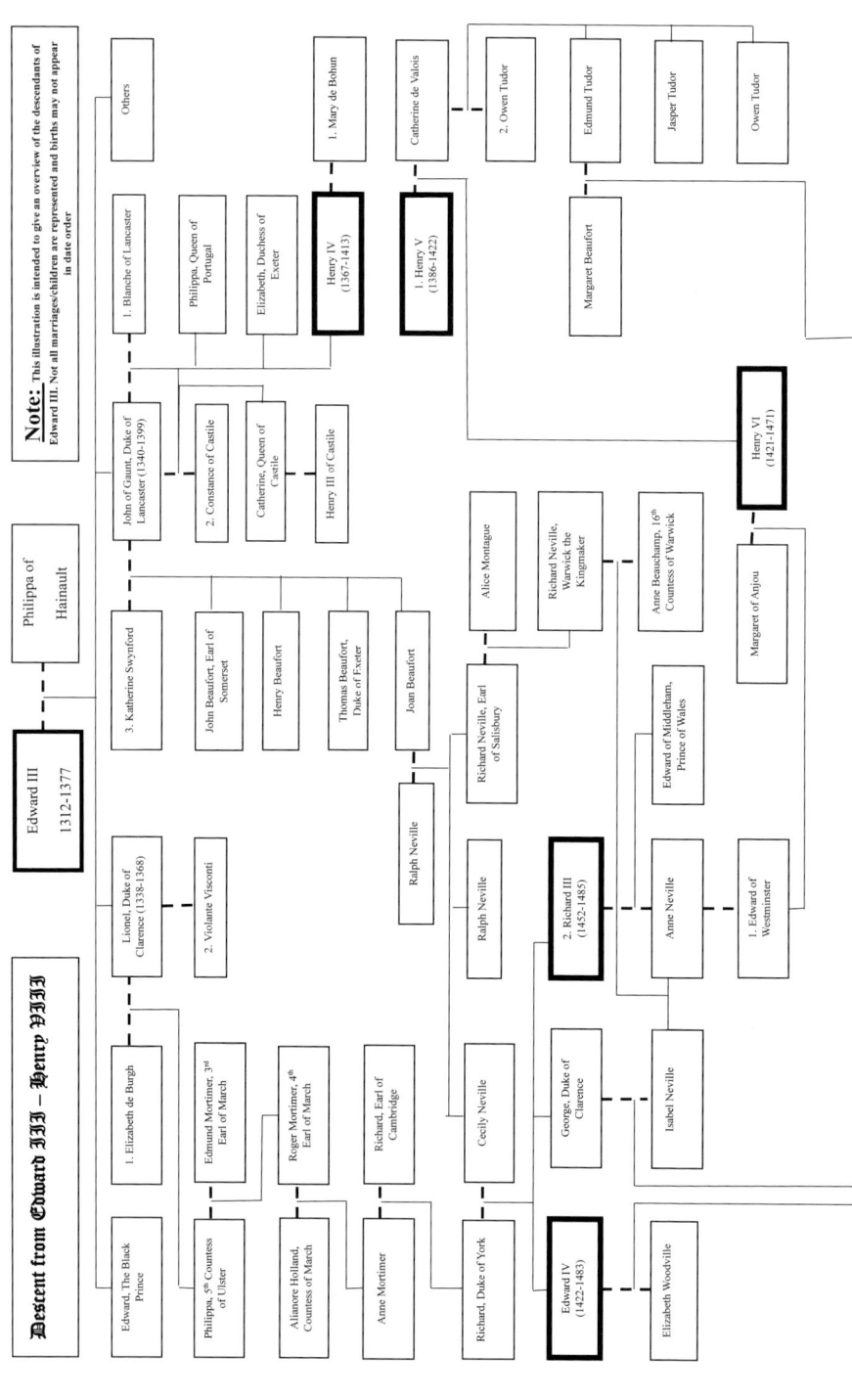

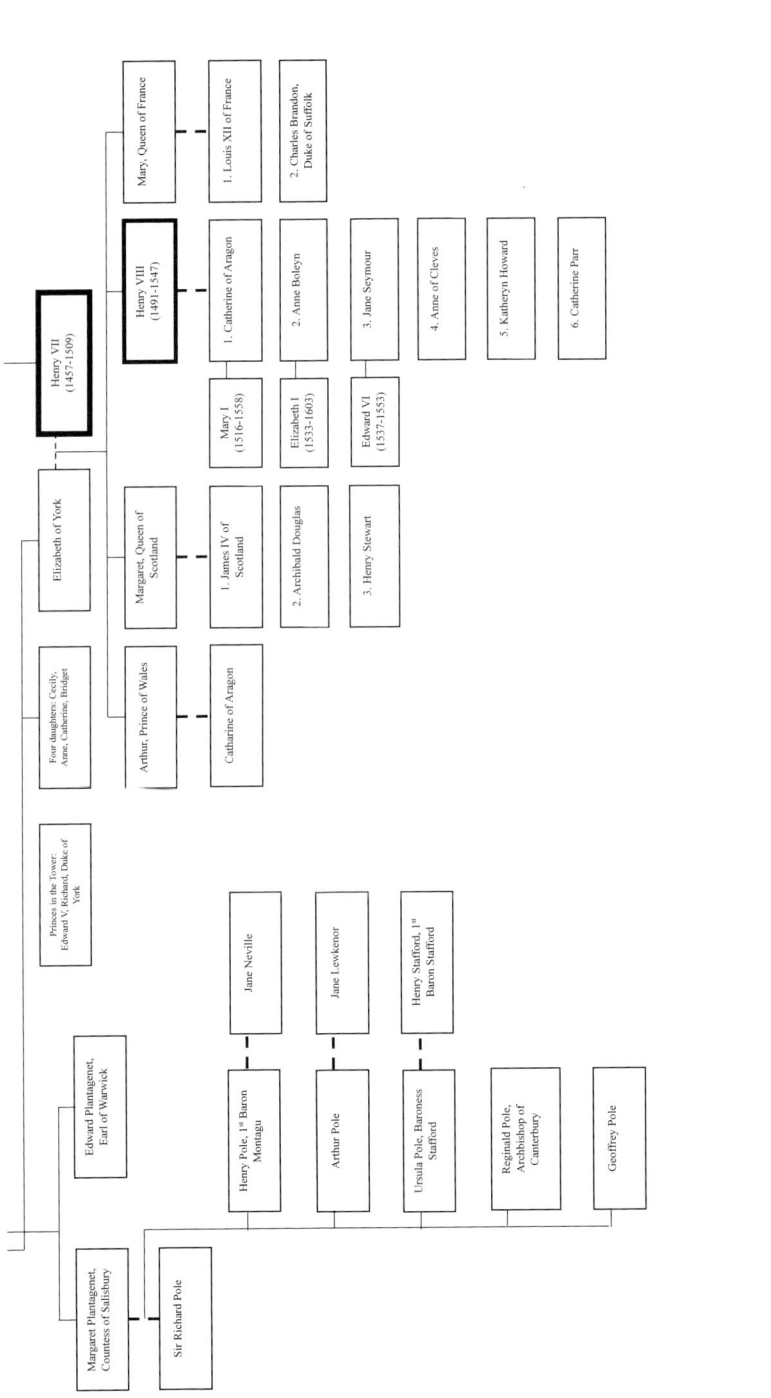

The Victorian stained-glass window in the Great Hall at Hampton Court Palace depicting Catherine of Aragon's descent from King Edward I and his first queen, Eleanor of Castile. (*Author's collection*)

Preface

Catherine of Aragon did not know she would become one of six very famous and influential queens; in fact, as far as she was concerned, she was the only Queen of England as the wife of King Henry VIII and she never wavered from this belief no matter what. She could have stepped aside and made life easier for herself and for her daughter Mary, but she could not take a course that she believed intrinsically to be wrong. She certainly would not stand aside and allow her husband to jeopardise his soul, so she fought until the very end to maintain the Roman Catholic Church in England, and her own rights and that of her daughter's. In a man's world, she stood out as a rare type of woman in a century that produced some quite extraordinary women around the world.

Nevertheless, she was not just extraordinary for her actions to save her marriage – like her successors she was extraordinary in her own right too. She was educated, well read, multilingual, pious, dutiful, generously charitable, loyal and politically astute. She proved herself a more than capable regent in Henry's stead and holds the distinction of being the first female ambassador in European history.

Catherine of Aragon was so much more than the wife Henry VIII divorced, and, by the end of this book, I think you will agree with Karen Lindsay's assessment of her in her excellent work *Divorced, Beheaded, Survived* (1995):

If Catherine of Aragon had been the eldest instead of the youngest daughter of Ferdinand and Isabella, she might be remembered not as the discarded consort of a marriage addicted king but as the powerful queen regnant of Spain, following in the footsteps of her formidable mother and altering the course of sixteenth-century European history.

A note on Catherine's name:
You may come across different versions of her name in this work. There wasn't standardised spelling in Catherine's lifetime and Catherine herself spelled her name in numerous ways. At birth she was named Catalina but has also been identified as Katherine, Katharine, Katherina, Katharina and even Kateryn by her daughter Mary.

Detail of a stained-glass window representing Catherine of Aragon. (*Giogo, Wikimedia, CC BY-SA 3.0; Public Domain image, via Wikimedia Commons*)

Chapter 1

Infanta of Spain

The Archiepiscopal Palace of Alcalá de Henares today; Catherine was born here. (*Fernando, Wikimedia, CC 4.0; Public Domain image, via Wikimedia Commons*)

Unlike some queens of England, we have a definitive date of birth for Catherine of Aragon, or Catalina as her parents named her; she was born on 16 December 1485 in the Archiepiscopal Palace of Alcalá de Henares.[1,2] Catherine came from quite a prestigious lineage; she could claim royal descent from Spain, Portugal and even her future kingdom of England via the House of Lancaster. One of Catherine's great-grandmothers on her mother's side was Catherine of Lancaster, a daughter of John of Gaunt, 1st Duke of Lancaster and his second wife, Constance of Castile. The earlier Catherine had married Enrique (Henry) III of Castile and the couple's only son Juan (John) was the father of Catherine's mother. It's possible Catherine was named in honour of her English great-grandmother; in fact, she appeared to inherit her fair complexion from her English ancestry too.[3]

Catherine was the last child born to her parents: the Catholic Monarchs of Spain, Isabella I of Castile and Ferdinand II of Aragon. One of the most powerful royal couples in history, Isabella and Ferdinand already had three daughters and a son, but unlike the future Henry VIII, Catherine's sex does not appear to have been a disappointment to them.

Catherine's mother, Isabella, was born on 22 April 1541 at the Madrigal de las Altas Torres, Avila, Castile, the eldest daughter of Juan II of Castile and his second wife, Isabel of Portugal. Her father had first been married to Maria of Aragon, with whom he had three children including Isabella's half-brother, the king of Castile.

Enrique (Henry) IV of Castile was widely regarded as a failure of a king. Nicknamed 'the Impotent', he preferred solitude and his animals to court life, refused to dress and behave like a king, and was a weak

A statue of a young Catherine, or Catalina as her parents named her, at the Archiepiscopal Palace of Alcalá de Henares. The statue was unveiled in 2007. (*Richard Mortel, Wikimedia, CC 2.0; Public Domain image, via Wikimedia Commons*)

man easily controlled by his nobles. This could, perhaps, all have been tolerated if he had produced an uncontested heir – but he didn't. His only child was the Princess Juana, born of his second marriage to Queen Juana of Portugal. The younger Juana is better known as *la Beltraneja*, as it was believed she was not the king's daughter at all but the daughter of Beltrán de la Cueva, a royal favourite at court. Rumours at the time imply that Enrique's nickname might have been a lot closer to home than generally realised, as he appears to have struggled to consummate both of his marriages.[4]

Whilst Isabella originally recognised the princess as heir to the throne, she soon became convinced (or allowed herself to be) that the princess was not her brother's daughter, and the true heir was her younger full brother, Alfonso. The young prince gathered a large following and on 5 June 1465 the 11-year-old was proclaimed king, whilst an effigy of Enrique was thrown from a mock throne into the dirt as a symbolic dethroning. It was the start of a civil war.⁵ Isabella supported Alfonso's cause, but tragically he died, aged just 14, on 5 July 1468. The rebels quickly turned to his elder sister, who instead of proclaiming herself queen, negotiated with Enrique and an agreement was reached where she promised not to marry without his consent but would also not be forced to marry and, perhaps most importantly, she was recognised as the heir to the throne in place of the princess Juana. Isabella was a lot of more politically astute than those around her – by supporting a fair, inherited succession and not uprooting the established order or fighting for the throne when the odds were against her, she hoped to guarantee a more stable and legitimate future for herself, her future heirs and her country and as the agreement was made on her own terms, she was not beholden or in the power of too many people.⁶

Catherine's mother, Isabella of Castile, by an unidentified artist, *c*.1490. Isabella was one of the most powerful queens of the sixteenth century and Catherine greatly admired her mother. The two were very similar in character and as she grew older many would comment on the fact that Isabella's youngest daughter was the most like her. (*Public Domain image, via Wikimedia Commons*)

Sadly, Enrique soon reneged on the terms of the agreement and insisted his daughter should inherit the throne. He held a ceremony in the Lozoya Valley where the nobles came to do homage to the 8-year-old princess, and he attempted to marry Isabella to Alfonso V of Portugal. Isabella, believing that the promises that had been made in good faith had been broken, decided instead to marry her second cousin, Ferdinand of Aragon, and the couple were wed in October 1469. The morning after their marriage, the bloodstained sheets were displayed to show the marriage had been consummated and that Isabella had been a virgin when she married.⁷ For the remainder of Enrique's life, an uneasy status quo was maintained with both sides continually trying to recruit supporters and showing signs of amicability, but both fully aware tensions lurked. Enrique died on 11 December 1474, and the day after Isabella was proclaimed Queen of Castile and Leon.

For the next four years the War of Castilian Succession would rage on with both sides making gains and suffering losses but the birth of Prince Juan (John) in 1478 to Isabella and Ferdinand consolidated Isabella's position and soon after an agreement was reached where the princess Juana was given two options: she could either wait to marry the newborn prince and become queen consort or enter a nunnery. She chose the latter.[8]

Catherine's father, Ferdinand, came from an equally interesting background. Born on 10 March 1452 and, like Isabella, born from his father, Juan (John) II of Aragon's, second marriage to Juana Enriquez, a Castilian noblewoman and a great-great-granddaughter of Alfonso XI of Castile.[9] Juan already had three surviving children from his first marriage to Blanche of Navarre, including a male heir, Ferdinand's half-brother Carlos (Charles), but the two had a very rocky relationship following Juan's refusal to hand over the kingdom of Navarre. The relationship worsened after his father's remarriage; Juana Enriquez appeared to regard her stepson as an interloper and understandably favoured her own son but less understandably encouraged his father to do so as well. Carlos died when Ferdinand was just 8 years old; it was rumoured he was poisoned but this was never officially proven.[10]

Catherine's father, Ferdinand of Aragon, by Michael Sittow, c.late fifteenth/early sixteenth century. Catherine would inherit much of her political ability from her father and she would prove a gifted pupil. (*Public Domain image, via Wikimedia Commons*)

A match between Isabella and Ferdinand had first been suggested when they were children and whilst his mother did not live to see it into fruition, his father did. Ferdinand had proved a loyal son and Juan had already gifted him Sardinia and Sicily and allowed him to use the title King of Sicily, but now he had an even more glorious future ahead of him as King of Castile and, in due course, Aragon as well.

Isabella and Ferdinand's first child, and Catherine's eldest sister was born on 2 October 1470,[11] just a year after her parents' marriage and was named after her mother. For eight years, Isabella would be the couple's only child as her parents were continually apart, attempting to defend the elder Isabella's right to her throne against the claims of the Princess Juana. As already noted, Prince Juan, Catherine's only brother, became Prince of Asturias and Girona, the titles held by the heir to the throne, upon his birth in 1478 on 30 June.[12] A second daughter named Juana (Joanna) after Ferdinand's mother was born on 6 November 1479,[13] followed by another daughter they named Maria, born on

Ferdinand and Isabella surrounded by their court. The youth to their right almost certainly is their son Don Juan, Prince of Asturias. The girls to their left may be their daughters. (*Public Domain image, via Wikimedia Commons*)

29 June 1482. Maria's birth was tinged with tragedy as she had been one of twins but only she survived; it is not clear if her twin sibling was a brother or a sister.[14]

With Catherine's birth the family was complete.

The few details we have of Catherine's first years were recorded by Isabella's treasurer, Gonzalo de Baeza. The new Infanta was christened by the Bishop of Pancia and for this special occasion she wore 'a gown of white brocade trimmed with gold lace and lined with green velvet'. Her maid was a lady called Elena de Carmona and like her siblings she travelled extensively as a child, in fact her first move took place within weeks of her birth though she would sometimes be left behind whilst her parents travelled on ahead or were needed elsewhere. There were a lot of happy reunions in Catherine's early years.[15]

Whilst the main figures in Catherine's life would have been her nurse and governess, her parents were not distant, unknowable figures; an English ambassador at Isabella and Ferdinand's court recorded that Isabella was very attentive to her daughter and he saw her hold Catherine up so that she could better see the tournaments taking place and noted they both were affectionate towards each other.[16] Isabella was the most influential woman in Catherine's entire life and later it would be realised that in character and temperament the Queen of Castile's youngest daughter was the one who most took after her.

6   Catherine of Aragon

Queen Isabella the Catholic, Presiding over the Education of her Children by Isidoro Lozanzo, c.1864. The little girl at the queen's lap likely represents Catherine. (*Public Domain image, via Wikimedia Commons*)

Isabella often lamented her own lack of education and was determined her daughters would not suffer the same fate. She appointed Humanist tutors that provided the four Infantas with the rigorous education they would need to ably perform their roles as princesses, duchesses, queens and perhaps empresses. Catherine was taught civil and canon law, scripture, history, classical and devotional literature and, most importantly for Isabella, Latin. As the main language of diplomacy, Isabella had had herself tutored in the language when she became queen by 'La Latina' Beatriz Galindo who would also teach her daughters.

Catherine was also taught the traditional feminine pursuits, which included sewing, embroidery, weaving, spinning, music, drawing and cooking. She was taught to dance by Portuguese tutors and thanks to her parents continual travelling was able to ride from a very young age; when she was older, she learnt falconry and how to hunt.

Isabella herself established a School of Classics and the aim of the school was to educate both young men and women so it needed both male and female tutors. Overseen by Pedro Martir, the male tutors included Fray Diego Deza and Lucio Marineo Siculus whilst the female tutors included a mathematician,

Alvara de Alba, the philosopher and linguist Cecilia Marello and the classicist and Erasmus disciple, Isabel de Vergara. Catherine may have benefitted from this school even if she did not attend all the lessons.

Catherine would have had access to her mother's extensive library, which included *Introduction to Latin and Castilian Grammar* by Antonia de Nebrija and *Universal Vocabulary in Latin and in Romance* by Alonso de Palencias and, most importantly, instruction manuals on how to raise daughters. Not all of Isabella books were for educational purposes; she also kept many chivalric stories and devotional works, which included the lives of saints.[17]

In 1490, Catherine had her first taste of a great state occasion when her eldest sister married the heir to the Portuguese throne, Prince Afonso. The proxy marriage took place in the Seville cathedral of Santa Maria de la Sede, where Catherine and her sisters were dressed in gold and jewels. Their sister's special day was followed by a two-week celebration that saw magnificent jousts and pageants. The younger Isabella was grandly escorted to Portugal and married her prince in the royal palace at Evora. What started as an arranged marriage developed into a rare love match as the prince and princess fell in love. Unusually for royal marriages, they had previously met when Isabella had lived in Portugal to honour the terms of the Treaty of Alcacovas that had been put in place to end the threat of Juana la Beltraneja.

The similarities between Isabella and Afonso's marriage and Catherine and Henry years later are striking. There was a five-year age difference between the bride and groom, both marriages started with the couple having met and knowing each other previously, both began as love matches and tragically both ended in tears. Just eight months after their marriage Prince Afonso died after being thrown from his horse and Isabella was grief-stricken by her loss. She refused to eat, cut her long hair and would only wear a sackcloth and veil. She vowed never to marry again and informed her parents of her desire to enter a religious life.[18]

However, perhaps the most important occasion for Catherine in her young life was the fall of Granada in 1492. The city was the last Moorish stronghold in Spain and Isabella and Ferdinand were determined to bring it under Spanish and Catholic rule. Catherine caught her first glimpse of it in 1489 when she and her family joined her father at Los Ojos de Huecar where he had based his army. Living in an army camp was not without its risks and one night the royal family had to be quickly evacuated when their tents caught fire. The fire destroyed most of the camp before it was eventually extinguished, though rather than an act of sabotage or a potential assassination plot it appears to have been a genuine accident caused by a candle that had been placed too close to a tapestry. The king and queen replaced the tents with houses of brick, not just

8 Catherine of Aragon

The Surrender of Granada by Francisco Pradilla y Ortiz, c.1882. (*Public Domain image, via Wikimedia Commons*)

as a safety precaution, but a sign that they were determined to see their course through, their armies having already taken back the cities of Marbella, Velez Malaga, Baza and Jaen amongst others.

In an interesting twist, the fall of Granada was helped along by a son of one of the last rulers, Abi Abdilehi, also known as Boabdil. He had rebelled against his unpopular father, styling himself Emir Muhammad XII, but had been captured by Isabella and Ferdinand's forces at Lucena where in return for his freedom he became their vassal and made war on his father. A Granadan chronicler commented that Boabdil's capture was 'the cause of the fatherland's destruction'. Boabdil soon became unhappy with the arrangement he had made, perhaps belatedly realising what he had helped set in motion or seeing that Castile would not allow him the power he craved, and he rebelled despite only holding Granada and the Alpujarras Mountains. He sent out increasingly desperate attempts for aid to, amongst others, the Sultan of Egypt and the Sultanate of Fes but as Granada was encircled by the armies of Castile no aid, if it was sent at all, was able to get through.

After an eight-month siege a provisional surrender, known as the Treaty of Granada, was signed by both sides on 25 November 1491. This was a short truce that guaranteed the rights of the Moors, including religious tolerance and fair treatment, in return for their surrender. The treaty also granted Jews the choice of either converting to Christianity or migrating to North Africa

The Alhambra Palace in Granada today. (*Jebulon, Wikimedia, CC1.0. Public Domain image, via Wikimedia Commons*)

within three years. The city finally surrendered on 2 January 1492 and four days later Isabella and Ferdinand entered Granada for the first time and visited the historic Alhambra Palace, a palace and fortress complex that had been the seat of the founder of the Emirate of Granada since 1238 and can still be seen in all its glory today.

The Reconquista of Spain was now complete.

It was at the Alhambra that the original Treaty of Granada was superseded by the Alhambra decree just a few months later. The decree ordered all Jews in Spain to choose between conversion or expulsion from Spanish territories. Isabella and Ferdinand were determined that their countries would be entirely Catholic but initially the aim was to gently convert those who remained through education and persuasion and Isabella appointed her confessor, Fernando de Talavera, as Archbishop of Granada for this purpose. This was a slow process and by 1499, the Bishop of Toledo, Franciso Jimenez de Cisneros, had lost all patience.

In 1478, Isabella and Ferdinand had initiated what would become known as the Spanish Inquisition which was intended to maintain Catholic orthodoxy

10   Catherine of Aragon

in their kingdoms, and under the inquisition Toledo would bring about many conversions and forced baptisms and it's not difficult to see why – the Spanish Inquisition would be one of the darkest periods of Spain's history. Jews were put into Ghettos, forced to leave the country and even buy their freedom if they could afford to do so. Converting could be a double-edged sword as conversos, as they were known, were still equally regarded with suspicion and hostility. Anyone could be a target – a person with a suspicious bloodline could be arrested, tortured and imprisoned. They were allowed no legal representation, did not know the charges against them, and a refusal to cooperate was an admission of guilt. Ironically, it was a descendant of a converted Jew, Tomas de Torquemada, who was appointed first Inquisitor General and it is estimated that he was responsible for between 2000–9000 deaths by formal execution and a further 100,000 perished in his dungeons; the true loss of life will never be known.[19]

Catherine was still a young child at this time, but she had been brought up to believe that Catholicism was the true faith, and she would be a true daughter of the Church all her life. Whilst the activities of the Inquisition make for horrific reading and the likely knowledge that Catherine would have seen nothing

The Return of Christopher Columbus after Eugene DelaCroix by an unknown artist c.1839. Columbus regaled Isabella and Ferdinand with tales of his adventures and Catherine may have heard them first hand. (*Public Domain image, via Wikimedia Commons*)

wrong with the processes can be difficult to acknowledge, we must remember that she was entirely a product of her time. Her parents would receive the title 'Catholic Monarchs' from the grateful Pope in 1494 for the completion of the Reconquista and the unification of Spain under the Catholic Church.

The Alhambra Palace would be the scene of another important event in Catherine's life. On 3 August 1492, funded by Isabella and Ferdinand, Christopher Columbus had set sail to discover a passage to India and China by sailing West rather than East, but instead he discovered an island in the Bahamas, which he named San Salvador (Holy Saviour). There he found a group of peaceful and friendly natives with gold jewellery who he believed would make good servants and be easily converted to Christianity. Horrifically he would take six of the inhabitants back to Spain as slaves but not before he landed in Cuba, Haiti and the Dominican Republic.

On his return, he attended the court of Isabella and Ferdinand and regaled them with tales of his travels and adventures. He told them of the islands he had visited, the storms he had endured, of new and exotic fruits, spices and flowers to be tried. The king and queen were delighted with his exploits and rewarded the explorer with titles and honours which included a new personal coat of arms and Columbus was soon planning his second voyage. Catherine may well have heard these tales first hand.[20]

Isabella and Ferdinand were at the pinnacle of their power and glory and with five children considered the most prized catches on the marriage market of Europe, they could afford to pick and choose the best partners for their son and daughters.

Chapter 2

Princess of Wales

Catherine was not even 3 years old when King Henry VII of England first showed a keen interest in her. His eldest son and heir, Prince Arthur, was just nine months younger than her, and with the Tudor dynasty in its infancy, acquiring a blue-blooded royal bride for him would be something of a diplomatic coup and show to the world that the Tudor dynasty was here to stay, as legitimate as any other royal house.

Henry made the first approach, issuing a commission to John Weston, Prior St John of Jerusalem in England; John Gunthorpe, Dean of Wells; Christopher Urswik, Great Almoner; and Thomas Savage and Henry Ainsworth, Doctors of Law to conclude a treaty of alliance with Ferdinand and Isabella, though they made no mention of a marriage proposal.[1] It must have been hinted at, however, as just a month later Ferdinand and Isabella in their turn commissioned their ambassador, Rodrigo Gonzalez de la Puebla, to conclude a marriage treaty between Catherine and Arthur.[2] Though Henry appears almost like a supplicant in this negotiation, a marriage alliance with England would draw benefits for Ferdinand and Isabella too. After years of hard work unifying their respective countries and the consolidation of power into their own hands, there was still one country that could pose a threat to Spain and her interests: France.

Catherine's father-in-law, King Henry VII of England, attributed to Meynnart Wewyck, c.1501–09. Henry was delighted to arrange his son's marriage to Catherine but their relationship would sour after Arthur's death. (*Public Domain image, via Wikimedia Commons*)

In 1462, France had seized the Aragonese provinces of Rousillon and Cerdagne from Ferdinand's father and Ferdinand had long desired their return, but he also hoped to add Naples to his existing Italian lands of Sardinia and Sicily, where France had also been making gains. By strange coincidence, the French and the English were long-term rivals and sometime enemies too. A marriage between Catherine and Arthur would provide another ally to help box France in; though the English Channel lay between the two countries, England did still control Calais which was based on French soil. It was not just a potential ally England and Spain could provide for each other but trade, shipping and security as well.

As with any marriage treaty, the most serious discussions that took place were over money. De Puebla met with his English counterparts, Richard Foxe, Bishop of Exeter and the diplomat, Giles Daubney, to negotiate the marriage portion and the jointure Catherine would be entitled to if Arthur predeceased her. Foxe and Daubney wanted three times the sum for the marriage portion that had been suggested when the original commissioners visited Spain, but De Puebla refused this as an outrageous request. The two men conceded and dropped their demand by half, but De Puebla would only agree a quarter. He may have been less than tactful in communicating his reason as to why he would not agree to such a large sum as originally suggested – he reportedly referred to the recent history of English kings and commented it was a wonder that Isabella and Ferdinand were considering agreeing to their daughter's marriage to Arthur at all.

De Puebla was referring to the recent civil war in England between two rival royal houses, now known as the Wars of the Roses, which had almost torn England apart over the previous thirty years. The war had seen the deposition and reinstating of two kings, the disappearance and likely murder of another and the death of one on the battlefield; the victor had been Henry VII.

Quite what Foxe and Daubney's reactions were to this pointed dig are unknown but the amount eventually agreed by both parties was 200,000 gold scudos. Catherine's jointure was set at a third of the revenue of Wales, Cornwall and Chester; Arthur had been Duke of Cornwall since his birth in 1486 but would be created Prince of Wales and Earl of Chester in November 1489. On 27 March 1489, the Treaty of Medina del Campo was signed between England and Spain; one part of the treaty was the arrangement of the marriage between Arthur and Catherine.

The marriage itself could not take place until both parties had reached the appropriate age – for girls this was 12 and for boys, 14, so Catherine would not leave her family for quite a few years. In the meantime, circumstances could change, and another match may be found for her that could be more beneficial to Spain.[3]

The next marriage to take place was Catherine's second eldest sister, Juana, to Archduke Philip of Burgundy in 1496. In keeping with their aim to marry their children for the benefit of Spain, the Dukedom of Burgundy was also on

Juana of Castile by Master of Affligem, c.1500. (*Public Domain image, via Wikimedia Commons*)

Juan Prince of Asturias and Girona from *The Madonna of the Catholic Monarchs* by an unknown artist, c.1491–1493. Catherine's only brother died young, devastating his family. (*Public Domain image, via Wikimedia Commons*)

the doorstep of France and had its own difficult relationship with that country. Philip was the son of Maximilian of Austria and Mary, Duchess of Burgundy. His mother was the only child of Duke Charles the Bold and when he died in 1477, the French King Louis XI had taken his chance to grab land that formerly belonged to Burgundy. This land had not been recovered but what was left was still a sizeable inheritance for Philip, which included the Netherlands and a dukedom with a rich history of culture and trade. An added benefit was that Maximilian and Mary had two children, and the second was a daughter, Margaret of Austria, who Ferdinand and Isabella thought would be the perfect spouse for their son and heir, Prince Juan.[4]

As with their eldest daughter, Isabella and Ferdinand ensured Juana was sent to Burgundy in style, with a magnificent trousseau including clothing and jewels that had been handpicked by both mother and daughter. It was not an easy journey with a freak wind destroying one of the ships in her escort, but she eventually arrived safely in her new kingdom, though her bridegroom did not arrive to greet her for several days. They were married on 20 October 1496;

the same fleet then escorted Margaret to her new home in Spain. She would also have to brave the stormy weather, but like Juana she also arrived safely in March 1497. The 11-year-old Catherine was with her parents to greet her at Santander.[5]

Juan and Margaret were married on 3 April 1497 in Burgos Cathedral, and it was immediately obvious that the two were captivated by each other. Margaret was witty, intelligent, beautiful and, most importantly, well educated – the perfect partner and future queen for her equally well-educated spouse, and she immediately ingratiated herself with her husband's family. Margaret became pregnant shortly after their marriage, but disaster struck when Prince Juan died suddenly on 4 October 1497 of an unknown illness. The only hope was the baby Margaret was carrying, but her pregnancy tragically ended in a miscarriage soon after. The loss of both her husband and unborn daughter devastated Margaret.

Prince Juan's death shook the royal family – Isabella and Ferdinand had lost their only son and heir and, amid family grief, had to look elsewhere to ensure their dynasty's survival. Luckily their eldest daughter had finally been persuaded

Margaret of Austria by Jean Hay, c.1490. (*Public Domain image, via Wikimedia Commons*)

Isabella, Princess of Asturias from *Madonna of the Catholic Monarchs* by an unknown artist, c.1491-1493. (*Public Domain image, via Wikimedia Commons*)

to marry again; Isabella married the king of Portugal, Manuel, just a month before her brother's death and was immediately recalled from Portugal to be sworn as the heiress presumptive. Isabella became pregnant shortly after her marriage, giving birth to her only son and heir, Miguel, in August 1498 but died shortly after. Her young son became the heir to his grandparents' thrones, but tragedy had not finished with Catherine's family yet, as his life was tragically cut short at just 2 years old in 1500; he died in his grandmother's arms.

In the space of a few short years, Catherine had lost a brother, a sister, a niece and a nephew. She would have seen and felt the same devastation her parents endured at so many losses, though she would not have questioned God's will. Now only she and her two sisters remained, and Juana was in Burgundy. Catherine would not have Maria's company for much longer as she married their elder sister's widower in 1500 to maintain the Portuguese alliance. As a result of Maria's departure, Catherine was the only child left with her parents and Isabella naturally clung to her youngest daughter, putting off her departure to England as long as she could, though at times she had more than one reason to do so.[6]

As early as 1493, Isabella and Ferdinand had broken the agreement with Henry VII by signing a treaty with the French king, Charles. Charles agreed to return the aforementioned lands taken from Ferdinand's father in return for which Isabella and Ferdinand had to agree not to marry any of their children into England. The breaking or amending of treaties, agreements and even marriage contracts was not unusual, and it may just have been a case of Catherine's parents keeping their options open or having no serious intention of honouring the new agreement with France. Apart from Arthur, there doesn't appear to have been another serious prospective bridegroom in mind for Catherine.

But there was a more troubling problem facing Catherine's potential marriage into England – would she have a throne to ascend?

Around this time, a man appeared claiming to be Richard, Duke of York, the rightful king of England. Richard, Duke of York, was the second son of Edward IV and one of the 'Princes in the Tower' who had vanished during the reign of Richard III. His elder brother, Edward V, became king on their father's death, but as he was still too young to rule, their father left instructions that Richard, Duke of Gloucester, his younger brother, should act as Lord Protector until he came of age. Richard instead declared his brother's marriage to the boys' mother, Queen Elizabeth Woodville, invalid, their children illegitimate and took the throne himself. The young princes, Edward and Richard, were last seen in the Tower of London during the summer of 1483. It was widely believed that Richard had ordered their deaths to remove any rivals to his throne and this belief led to a major loss of support for the new king and many

The Children of Edward by Paul Delaroche, c.1830. The brothers of Queen Elizabeth of York, Edward V and Richard, Duke of York were last seen alive at the Tower of London and whilst there are many theories surrounding their fate, their disappearance has never been solved. (*Public Domain image, via Wikimedia Commons*)

transferred their loyalties to Edward and Elizabeth's surviving daughters. Their eldest daughter was Elizabeth of York, but despite her popularity a woman had never successfully ruled England and so her supporters looked to the last heir of the house of Lancaster, Henry, Earl of Richmond.

Henry was the only son of Lady Margaret Beaufort, Countess of Richmond and her first husband Edmund Tudor, Earl of Richmond. Edmund was a half-brother of the ill-fated, Lancastrian King Henry VI, via their shared mother – the French princess and queen of Henry V, Catherine of Valois. Margaret herself was the daughter and sole heiress of John Beaufort, Duke of Somerset, a legitimised grandson of John of Gaunt, 1st Duke of Lancaster by his mistress, later third wife, Katherine Swynford. Henry's claim to the throne was tenuous to say the least, but an agreement was reached where he would invade England, take the throne from the unpopular Richard III and marry Elizabeth of York, thereby uniting the rival houses of York and Lancaster and ending the so-called Wars of the Roses that had plagued England for generations.

Henry successfully invaded in 1485, defeating and killing Richard at Bosworth and becoming King Henry VII, ushering in the Tudor dynasty. He married Elizabeth in 1486. Some people believed he delayed the marriage to ensure people did not think he ruled via right of his wife, but it is equally possible, as Elizabeth and her sisters had been declared illegitimate, he was forced to wait while the necessary legislation was revoked to re-legitimise the children of Edward IV and Elizabeth Woodville, thereby ensuring any children they had together in the future would not be tainted by the stigma.

The problem Henry VII had was that if his wife was legitimate then her brothers, the missing princes were too. If they were found or reappeared, they would be the true heirs to the throne of England. To this day it has never been conclusively explained what happened to the boys, which left an opening for imposters or perhaps even the real boys to make a claim to the throne which is exactly what happened.

Henry had already seen off one pretender in 1487 but this new claimant would be more problematic. Known today as Perkin Warbeck, he managed to attract the support of some well-known European figures including the Holy Roman Emperor Maximilian, King James IV of Scotland and Margaret, the Dowager Duchess of Burgundy. Margaret's recognition was perhaps the most dangerous of all as she was a sister of the princes' father. By coincidence, Maximilian was also Margaret's stepson in law[7] and the pair had a close bond. He supplied fourteen ships for Warbeck to invade England but the invasion ended in failure. Warbeck spent the 1490s travelling between Europe, Ireland and Scotland, seeking support for his claims and causing difficulties for Henry VII along the way, before he was finally captured after landing in Cornwall in 1497. After confessing to being an imposter, he was treated well by Henry, but an escape attempt eight months after his surrender saw him recaptured and thrown into the Tower of London. He was later accused of trying to escape with the already imprisoned 17th Earl of Warwick, though there is some suspicion surrounding this plot.

Portrait of an Infanta, possibly Catherine of Aragon, by Juan de Flandes, c.1496. Infanta is a royal title used by the children of reigning and past Spanish monarchs and the children of the heir to the Crown. (*Public Domain image, via Wikimedia Commons*)

The 17th Earl of Warwick was Edward Plantagenet, the only son of George

Plantagenet, Duke of Clarence and his wife, Isabel Neville. George was the brother of Edward IV and Richard III and a potential claimant to the English throne, but following his conviction and execution for treason, his son Edward was considered disbarred. But that did not stop plots springing up around him, and so upon Henry's accession he immediately had Warwick confined in the Tower.

However, if Henry was so worried about his throne and his family, why were Warbeck and Warwick not kept more closely guarded? How were they able to plot an escape? One theory suggests that the second escape attempt was set in motion by Henry and his councillors to give Henry a legitimate reason to be rid of two troublesome potential claimants.

It was not just Henry's own dynasty he was concerned about; it had been suggested to him that Catherine's parents would hardly allow their daughter to travel to a country where she could not be sure of her throne and safety. Both men were executed in November 1499 and afterwards the Spanish Ambassador wrote to Isabella and Ferdinand:

> *Now that Perkin and the son of the Duke of Clarence have been executed, there does not remain 'a drop of doubtful royal blood', the only Royal blood being the true blood of the King, the Queen and, above all, the Prince of Wales.*[8]

Whilst nothing survives today to indicate this was a condition of Catherine coming to England, that does not mean to say verbal messages were not passed between the ambassadors and the monarchs. Interestingly, Catherine herself believed it was done on her behalf and carried a lot of guilt with this knowledge. Warwick's nephew, Cardinal Reginald Pole, later wrote the below account and there is no reason to doubt its accuracy. He was the Earl of Warwick's nephew through his mother, Margaret Pole, who became a close friend and confidante of Catherine:

> *I will tell you of the grievous trouble and remorse which his majesty's aunt, the most Serene Queen Katherine, had to endure, as frequently alluded to by herself, always thinking of this, namely, that a great part of her trouble emanated from god, not through any fault of her own, but for the salvation of her soul; and that the Divine justice thus punished the sin of her father King Ferdinand, for when he commenced negotiating her marriage with Prince Arthur, the eldest son of the King of England, some disturbances took place at the time, owing to the favour and goodwill borne by the people to my mother's brother the Earl of Warwick, of whom we have made mention above, who being the son of the Duke of Clarence, brother of King Edward, became, by the death of that Kings sons,*

> next heir to the English crown. King Ferdinand, having by the agreements to conclude his daughters marriage at that time, made a difficulty about it, saying he would not give her to one who was not secure in his own kingdom; and thus, by inciting the King to do what already desired spontaneously, he was the cause of the death of that innocent Earl, who had no more blame in those commotions, nor could anything else be laid to his charge, save the danger which the King in Council had alleged had already befallen him in part, through the existence of the said Earl; and in addition to this having heard the opinion of the King of Spain, he did that deed, of winch (as I have already said) he so greatly repented on his deathbed.[9]

In January 1497, an amended version of the Treaty of Medina del Campo was signed by both Catherine and her parents, a sure indication that Catherine was now a young woman and ready to proceed to the next stage of her life. The formal betrothal took place on 15 August 1497 at Woodstock Palace, Oxfordshire, but it was not until 19 May 1499 at a ceremony held at Tickenhill Manor in Worcestershire, that Catherine and Arthur were married by proxy, with the Spanish ambassador, Rodrigo Gonzalez de la Puebla, standing in for Catherine. The ceremony took place at around nine in the morning following Mass; the ambassador joined hands with Arthur and spoke her vows to which Arthur responded:

> ... he was very much rejoiced to contract with Catherine ...in indissoluble marriage, not only in obedience to the Pope and King Henry, but also for his deep and sincere love for the princess, his wife.[10]

The ceremony was followed by a great banquet in which the ambassador was served the best dishes and given the seat of honour. Catherine was now officially the Princess of Wales or 'la Princessa de Gales'[11] as she was known in her native Spain.

What is interesting is that the couple had been writing to each other since at least the summer of 1498. Whilst this doesn't seem unusual to us, it was not a common occurrence for future royal spouses at the time. If it was felt that anything important needed to be passed on, this was done through official channels – for example, when de Puebla wrote to Catherine, informing her that her mother-in-law had advised her to converse in French as often as possible with her sister-in-law to learn the language as the ladies in England did not understand Latin or Spanish.[12] Catherine was also asked to accustom herself to drinking wine as the water in England was not drinkable.[13]

It's not known who first suggested they should write or even who sent the first letter, but it laid the foundation for these two young strangers to build their relationship and may even have aided diplomacy between the two countries in a more subtle way. Sadly, we know of only one letter that survives from their correspondence. Written by Arthur to Catherine, it is dated 5 October 1499 and refers to his hope to have her by his side soon:

Most illustrious and most excellent lady, my dearest spouse, I wish you very much health, with my hearty recommendation.

I have read the most sweet letters of your highness lately given to me, from which I have easily perceived your most entire love to me. Truly those your letters, traced by your own hand, have so delighted me, and have rendered me so cheerful and jocund, that I fancied I beheld your highness and conversed with and embraced my dearest wife. I cannot tell you what an earnest desire I feel to see your highness, and how vexatious to me is this procrastination about your coming. I owe eternal thanks to your excellence that you so lovingly correspond to this my so ardent love. Let it continue, I entreat, as it has begun; and, like as I cherish your sweet remembrance night and day, so do you preserve my name ever fresh in your breast. And let your coming to me be hastened, that instead of being absent we may be present with each other, and the love conceived between us and the wished-for joys may reap their proper fruit.

Moreover I have done as your illustrious highness enjoined me, that is to say, in commending you to the most serene lord and lady the king and queen my parents, and in declaring your filial regard towards them, which to them was most pleasing to hear, especially from my lips. I also beseech your highness that it may please you to exercise a similar good office for me, and to commend me with hearty good will to my most serene lord and lady your parents; for I greatly value, venerate, and esteem them, even as though they were my own, and wish them all happiness and prosperity.

May your highness be ever fortunate and happy, and be kept safe and joyful, and let me know it often and speedily by your letters, which will be to me most joyous. From our castle of Ludlow. 5th of October, 1499.

Your highness' most loving spouse,
Arthur, Prince of Wales, Duke of Cornwall, etc.
Eldest son of the King.[14]

After a series of issues including illness, rebellion in Granada and bad weather, Catherine finally bid her parents farewell on 21 May 1501. This must have been an extremely difficult and painful moment for the young Catherine as she knew it was unlikely she would ever see her parents or homeland again and she was only 15. Whilst this was not an unusual age for a princess of this time to leave home, even for another country, and Catherine had been raised to expect this and to do her duty to her family, after the series of tragedies and losses they had faced, it would be most unusual if Isabella, Ferdinand and Catherine hadn't become a lot closer as a result. Isabella had certainly been reluctant to see her youngest child go and whilst Ferdinand was not given to extreme displays of emotion, it's not to say he was unfeeling – though in a few years his relationship with Juana would prove to be very complicated for both personal and political reasons.

Catherine departed with a household of 55 people to serve her including maids, cooks, cupbearers, bishops, knights and archers. Isabella had originally planned to send a household of around 150, but Henry objected, rightly worrying that Catherine would be unable to integrate into English life and customs with such a large Spanish household around her. Isabella had also wanted to accompany her daughter on part of her journey to England, escorting her as far as the port of Coruña where she would embark, but her own ill health had necessitated her remaining in Granada. In total, Catherine's journey to Coruña would take her three months; whilst Catherine was travelling as fast as she could, the heat would not allow for long journeys.

On the way she visited the monastery at Guadalupe and was feasted by the citizens of Zamora. She then travelled through Toleda and Valladolid and made her way to Santiago de Compostela where she visited the cathedral as a pilgrim to see the reputed tomb of St James. By the middle of August she had arrived at Coruña. On 17 August her ships attempted to set sail for England, but stormy weather damaged the hulls and sails, forcing their return to port; it would not be until 27 September that Catherine would depart her country, never to see it again.

The weather was not finished with her yet, as soon after the storms returned and would continue to plague her journey every few hours for the next six days. Once they had travelled through the Bay of Biscay and around Brittany, they entered the English Channel where they docked at Plymouth on 2 October. The nightmarish sea journey was finally over, and Catherine had arrived in her new home.[15] Whilst Catherine was used to travelling on land, this was her first voyage at sea and we don't know if she suffered any ill effects from it, but she did ask upon disembarking to be taken to the local church to give thanks for her safe arrival.

The next day Catherine set off for Exeter, where on the 19 October she received a delegation of English nobles and a letter of welcome from her father-in-law. She was treated with every courtesy and splendidly entertained. As soon as news spread of her arrival, other English men and women rushed to greet

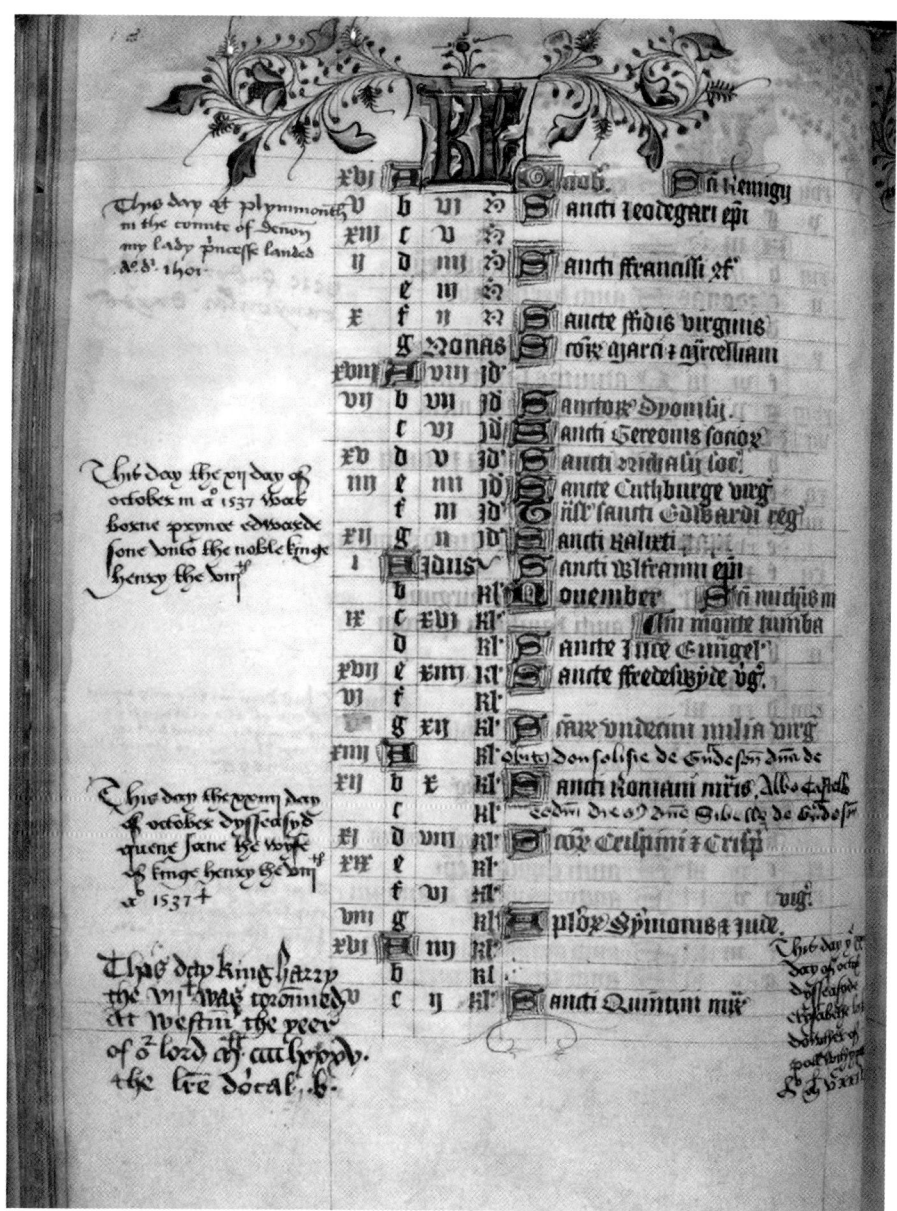

A Page from *The Beaufort / Beauchamp Hours*; the top left inscription records Catherine's arrival in England. (*Public Domain image, via Wikimedia Commons*)

their future queen and to present her with gifts. On 6 November, Catherine arrived at Dogmersfield House in Hampshire where, unbeknown to her, the first test of her skills in diplomacy was to take place.[16]

Henry had grown impatient to meet his daughter-in-law and to see if she was all he had been led to believe. When he was informed she had landed, he set off shortly after his delegation to greet her; Arthur also left Ludlow Castle and met his father enroute. When the king and prince arrived, Catherine's household was thrown into chaos. Her parents had insisted Catherine was not to be seen or communicate with her husband and his family until the wedding day, she was even required to remain veiled. Henry, annoyed by the barriers erected, immediately consulted his councillors who advised him that as Catherine was now on English soil, Spanish jurisdiction did not apply, and that he was well within his rights to meet and greet her. When Henry tried to insist upon greeting her Catherine's duenna, Elvira Manuel, who was the equivalent of an English governess, was horrified and insisted Catherine was already in bed, to which Henry replied he would greet her there if that was so.

A portrait of a young noble woman by Michael Sittow, c.1514. Long believed to be a portrait of Catherine as a young woman, its identity has recently been questioned. (*Public Domain image, via Wikimedia Commons*)

As a tense stalemate approached, Catherine amicably agreed to greet the king, asking only for a little time to make herself ready. Once she was so, Catherine met her father-in-law for the first time.[17] As a young woman Catherine was described as having red-gold colouring, pale skin, pink cheeks, rosebud lips and blue eyes.[18] She was short but had a slight plumpness that indicated she would be fertile.[19] Contemporary English standards of beauty were almost exactly this, so Catherine was exactly what the people of England had hoped for.

Immediately after greeting the king, Catherine came face to face with Arthur for the first time. What they thought of each other is not recorded but each had been brought up to consider the other as their future husband/wife respectively so there would have been no difficulties there, though Catherine would not have expected to come face to face with him so soon. They had communicated via letter but neither could understand the other without the help of translators, so actual conversation may have been limited. Whilst the king retired, Arthur remained with Catherine whose minstrels played for them. Both danced but not with each other as this would have been wildly inappropriate prior to their marriage, but they also knew very different styles of dance.

Soon after, Henry and Arthur departed for London where they could oversee the celebrations prepared for Catherine's arrival, Catherine followed at a more leisurely pace. She was escorted by the Duke of Buckingham, Edward Stafford, whom she had met at Kingston upon Thames. Just outside the city of London, Catherine met another member of her new family – her brother-in-law, Henry Duke of York, who was to escort her through the city.[20]

London had been transformed in Catherine's honour. The streets were decorated and music played and before long she was greeted by a figure representing St Catherine, declaring that she had watched over the princess since she was born and would oversee her entry into London. St Catherine was joined by St Ursula who reminded Catherine of her Lancastrian heritage which she shared with her future husband.

The saints now escorted her to the first of six magnificent pageants that lined the way to greet her. Pageants at this time held a lot of significance: they were religious, political, moral and amusing. The first pageant represented the Castle of Policy and offered Catherine advice on how to rule with Arthur and to do so honourably. The second pageant focussed on the union of the red rose of Lancaster and the white rose of York, as represented firstly by Arthur's parents and more so by Arthur's birth. The third pageant depicted one of Catherine's ancestors, King Alfonso the Wise of Castile, prophesying that the young couple's marriage would be blessed with many children as it had been foretold in the stars that a 'goodly pryncess young and tender would marry a noble prince'. It also reminded her of her higher allegiance to God, something which Catherine would never forget. The fourth pageant showed Arthur as the Sun King who shone brightly and dispensed wisdom and justice. The fifth was titled 'The Temple of God' with comparisons made between King Henry and the Lord and a speech on the holy union of marriage. At St Paul's Cathedral the last pageant depicted the seven cardinal virtues: faith, hope, charity, justice, temperance, prudence and fortitude of strength. Two empty seats waited to receive Catherine and Arthur. Here Catherine was greeted by the Mayor, aldermen and guildsmen who presented her with the traditional gifts of basins and pots filled with coins. Catherine thanked them sincerely before entering the cathedral, where she received the blessing of the Archbishop of Canterbury and left an offering to St Erkenwald. She was then escorted to the Bishop of London's Palace where she could rest and prepare for another long day ahead. Catherine had been secretly observed on her procession by the king and queen, Arthur and Margaret Beaufort; none had wanted to detract from the princess' special day, but all were keen to observe the proceedings and ensure nothing went wrong.[21]

Old St Paul's Cathedral from *Early Christian Architecture* by Francis Bond (1913). Prince Arthur and Catherine were married in the cathedral but they would not recognise St Paul's as it looks today as it was largely destroyed during the fire of London. From a copy in the possession of Mr Crace, Esquire, of the earliest known view of London, taken by Van der Wyngarde for Philip II of Spain. Catherine's daughter, Mary Tudor, married Philip II of Spain in 1556. (*Public Domain image, via Wikimedia Commons*)

The morning of 14 November was a hive of activity. St Paul's Cathedral was beautifully decorated with 'the moost excellent ornementes apperteynynyng unto the worship of God and honour of this joyfull maryage and union of the most reverent prince and princes'. Jewels, relics and plate were displayed on every surface to show the Tudors wealth and power. Despite this day being one of the most important days in Tudor royal history, the day was entirely about Catherine herself. The Spanish nobility proceeded into the cathedral first, walking two by two and arm in arm alongside 'a goodly multitude of estatis lords and gentilmen in their araye and ordre'. Catherine arrived at St Paul's escorted by her brother-in-law. For her wedding she was dressed magnificently in white satin with a coif on her head of white silk and a border of gold, pearl and precious stone. An elegant veil fell from the coif to her middle, covering, 'great part of her visage'. Her train was carried by her husband's aunt, Cecily of York, who was herself followed by Catherine's ladies and gentlewomen. Arthur also wore a garment of white satin so the young couple would have complemented each other.

It appeared that the groom's parents were absent but there was a good reason. As it was their son's special day, royal convention dictated that the prince and princess should not be upstaged or outranked by the king and queen of England, but Henry and Elizabeth would not miss such an important occasion for both

Princess of Wales 27

North facade of Westminster Abbey. Prince Arthur and Catherine showed themselves to the crowds gathered here and were greeted with rapturous applause. (*Author's Collection*)

their son and their dynasty; they witnessed the entire ceremony discreetly through a window from a closet above.

Before the religious ceremony could take place, the business side had to be dealt with. Henry's councillors declared that the union was the will of the kings of England and Spain and announced the amount Henry was due for Catherine's marriage portion. Catherine was then given the letters patent that confirmed her jointure. Now that the business had been dealt with, the religious ceremony could begin. The ceremony was performed by the Archbishop of Canterbury, Henry Deane. Surprisingly for such an important occasion we don't have a detailed description of the service, only that the archbishop did 'conjoynne their noble persons toguyder as the custom and sacrament in this bhealve doeth require and aske'. Arthur then escorted Catherine to both the North and South doors so that they could be seen by the multitude that had gathered. They were well rewarded for their consideration as the crowd erupted in cheers and applause upon seeing them. The newly married couple returned to the altar to hear the Mass of the Trinity before exiting via the West door where they were greeted by Catherines seventh pageant: a green mountain covered in trees and herbs flowing with wine. They then walked to the palace of the Bishop of London for their wedding feast. A chamber had been decorated with 'every annowrement that might belonge to so noble estate' and a great feast of venison, fish and plenty of wine of was provided.

Whilst the celebrations were in full swing the Great Chamberlain – John de Vere, Earl of Oxford – and the Duchess of Norfolk and the Countess of Cambria departed to prepare the marital bed to receive the newlyweds. The chamber they were to use was inspected and both sides of the bed tested to ensure nothing had been hidden in the mattress that could harm the couple. Catherine was the first to leave the celebrations and was escorted to the chamber where she was ceremoniously prepared and helped into bed, Arthur arrived soon after. The bishops blessed the bed and refreshments were left for the couple to enjoy before everyone departed and they were left to consummate their marriage.[22]

What happened that night would become one of the most hotly debated topics in royal history.

Chapter 3

Uncertain Times

The day after her marriage Catherine enjoyed a well-deserved rest in her chambers closeted with her ladies, and only received the Earl of Oxford who delivered a message and a gift from the king. But the celebrations for Catherine and Arthur's marriage lasted nearly two weeks. Two days after their marriage, the young couple returned with the nobility to St Paul's Cathedral to attend a Mass offering and Catherine had an audience with her father-in-law in which they met with 'right pleasant and favourable words, greetings and communications.'[1] The day after was the ceremonial dubbing of the new Knights of the Bath which was followed by jousts, pageants, banquets and dancing that ran well into the week after.

Amongst all these magnificent celebrations, Catherine had to endure a sad parting. She had known that not all her household would remain with her forever but when the day came for some to return to Spain she was noticeably saddened and understandably homesick. She would have less support from her own people going forward and must have felt isolated in a new land whose customs and language she did not yet understand. The king took it upon himself to cheer her up by showing her his extensive library of Latin works and then presenting her with his jeweller, who brought with him rings and precious stones which Henry told Catherine and her ladies that they could each pick one to keep for themselves. This appeared to help and Catherine 'assuaged her heaviness and drew herself into the manner, guise and usages of England'.[2]

However, another incident took place in which the king would not come across in such a good light. Henry had been promised an extra 35,000 scudos for Catherine's dowry in the shape of gold, silver, jewels and tapestries but so far this had not appeared. It seems De Puebla encouraged Henry to ask for these items from Catherine's own possessions in recompense – this would later mean they could not be included as part of her dowry. But Catherine's Master of Wardrobe, Juan de Cuero, refused and stated that her property was to remain in Spanish possession and that he was to weigh, value and guard them and that he would require a receipt. Quite why De Puebla was trying to extort more money from his king and queen in favour of the English king is unknown but Henry was deeply embarrassed by this episode as it made him come across as grasping and miserly. He felt the need to explain himself to Catherine and asked her to write to her parents to explain De Puebla's crafty scheme.³

Arthur and Catherine remained at court until 21 December, when they departed for Arthur's seat at Ludlow Castle. There had been some debate as to whether Catherine was to accompany her husband or not, giving some evidence to the claim that Arthur's health was frail at this time. Too much sex at a young age was believed to be bad for the male partner and it was widely believed to have played a factor in Catherine's own brother's death in 1497. Henry had originally wanted his son to consummate his marriage, therefore making it legal in the eyes of the Church and then have him return to Ludlow whilst Catherine remained at court with the king and queen until they were both older.

Arthur Prince of Wales by the Anglo Flemish School, *c.*1500. The only known portrait of the prince painted during his lifetime. (*Public Domain image, via Wikimedia Commons*)

Ludlow Castle. (*Andrew Hackney, Wikimedia CC 2.0; Public Domain image, via Wikimedia Commons*)

Both Henry and Arthur's councillors and Catherine's confessor disagreed with this whilst the Spanish ambassador and some members of Catherine's household supported the idea. Arthur was even prompted to ask Catherine what she herself wanted but she diplomatically agreed to go along with whatever the king thought best: 'neither in this nor in any other respect had she any other will than his, and that she would be content with whatever he decided'. After much thought, Henry concluded that Catherine would go to live with her husband. His decision may have been influenced by De Puebla's earlier scheme.

What seems strange is that no plans appear to have been made for Catherine's household in Wales. When Duenna Elvira Manuel made enquiries, she discovered that it had been the responsibility of De Puebla to organise and that he had made repeated assurances of this to Catherine's parents that this was in hand, but now he claimed this was entirely news to him. If Catherine now went to live with Arthur she would have to use her own jewels and plate for her expenses, thereby devaluing it and making it unacceptable as part of her dowry and the king would be able to claim more money or jewels from Spain.[4]

It would take until around the new year for Catherine and Arthur to arrive at Ludlow Castle. As they approached, the townsfolk and local magnates lined the way to greet their future queen and in the great hall of Ludlow Castle, Catherine was greeted by her husband's household before being escorted to her chambers, which were situated in the north-west side of the castle. The couple had separate chambers as was usual and it would be Arthur's responsibility to initiate marital relations with his wife.

We don't have a lot of detail for Catherine's activities whilst at Ludlow; it is probable that she used her time there ingratiating herself with her new people, learning the language and customs of England and most importantly establishing a relationship with her husband when he was not occupied with his duties. In years to come it would be proven how warmly Catherine had been accepted, but even as early as 1501 she made a lifelong friend in Margaret Pole, the future Countess of Salisbury, despite what must have been an uncomfortable beginning. Margaret was the wife of Arthur's chamberlain, Sir Richard Pole, but she was also the sister of the executed Earl of Warwick and only daughter of George Duke of Clarence, niece to Edward IV and Richard III, and cousin of the current queen. Margaret's closeness to the throne had caused her no end of problems and would continue to do so in the future, but for now, married to a Tudor loyalist she was treated as an extended member of the family.

On 24 March, Arthur celebrated Maundy Thursday. He distributed money and alms to the poor of the region and perhaps, as was traditional, washed their feet; it was his last public engagement.[5] By the end of March, both Catherine and Arthur fell ill with what was suspected at the time to be the sweating sickness or

A tapestry in the Flemish style believed to depict the court of Arthur, Prince of Wales and his wife Catherine of Aragon, artist unknown, c.1500s. (*Public Domain image, via Wikimedia Commons*)

the plague, but opinions differ to this day. Whatever the sickness was, Catherine would recover; Arthur would not. Arthur died on 2 April 1501, just five months after their marriage. After his death his body was carefully examined and one doctor diagnosed 'tisis' or 'phthisis' as the cause of the prince's death. 'Tisis' and 'phthisis' were terms for pulmonary tuberculosis.

Arthur's council dispatched an urgent messenger to the king and queen and upon receiving the dreadful news Henry sent for Elizabeth so that they could 'take the painfull sorrows together'. Elizabeth immediately started to comfort her husband telling him that they were still young and could have more children and that they still had a prince and two princesses. Shortly after her own grief hit her and the king in turn comforted his devastated wife.[6]

We don't know when Catherine was made aware of the tragedy that had taken place but she was not present at Arthur's funeral. This was due to royal protocol, but it's not known how ill Catherine herself was at this time, so she may not have been well enough to attend even if she had wanted too. Arthur's funeral took place on 25 April 1501 and he was laid to rest in Worcester Cathedral; his heart and bowels had been removed and buried in the Ludlow Chapel of St Mary Magdalene. His beautiful tomb and Chantry Chapel at Worcester can still be seen today.

Arthur, Prince of Wales memorial plaque in St Mary's Chapel at Ludlow. (*Philip Halling, Geograph Britain and Ireland, Wikimedia, CC2.0; Public Domain image, via Wikimedia Commons*)

Upon her recovery, Catherine donned the black mourning clothing of a widow and waited to hear what would happen next. Catherine's fate was not her own, it lay in the hands of her parents and father-in-law. She was now a widow in a strange land, she had no close family to turn to for advice and the future she had been brought up to believe was hers all her life was now in ruins …or was it?

Upon learning of Arthur's death, Catherine's parents immediately wrote to Henry and requested her return to Spain, but this is not what they truly wanted. Arthur's younger brother, Henry Duke of York, was now the

Prince Arthur's tomb in his Chantry Chapel at Worcester Cathedral. (*Hugh Llewelyn, Wikimedia, CC 2.0; Public Domain image, via Wikimedia Commons*)

Margaret Tudor by an unknown artist, c. sixteenth century. Margaret was the eldest daughter of King Henry VII and Queen Elizabeth of York. (*Public Domain image, via Wikimedia Commons*)

Elizabeth of York by an unknown artist, c.1530. Catherine's mother-in-law, her early death left Catherine without an important ally and protector during her first few years in England. (*Public Domain image, via Wikimedia Commons*)

heir to the throne, and he would also require a wife and who better than a Spanish princess he was already acquainted with and available to him?[7] Both sides wanted to maintain the alliance that had been promised with Arthur and Catherine's marriage and Henry was equally reluctant to return the portion of Catherine's dowry he had received, but there was the problem of consanguinity. The Pope would need to provide a dispensation to allow a marriage between Henry and Catherine as they were now related within the forbidden degree as brother and sister-in-law. There was also the question of consummation and pregnancy. Catherine insisted she was still a virgin and that she and Arthur had not consummated their marriage and had, in fact, spent only around seven nights of their whole married life together.

Whilst these discussions were taking place, Queen Elizabeth organised Catherine's return to London. She arrived in June, carried in a black velvet fringed litter and was settled into her new residence at Durham House which was to be her home for the next three years. As it was a household in mourning, Catherine lived a quiet life seeing very few people, though she did receive gifts and books from the queen. It would not to be until November that she visited

Presentation page from the *Vaux Passional*, Peniarth MS 482 D, f. 9r, *c.*1503–04. This illuminated miniature depicts King Henry VII and his children in mourning for Elizabeth of York. Margaret and Mary Tudor are on the left and the future Henry VIII weeps beside an empty bed. (*Public Domain image, via Wikimedia Commons*)

the court, travelling in the queens barge to and from Westminster. She is not recorded as attending the Christmas festivities that year.[8]

There were a few factors occurring at this time that meant Catherine was not a high priority for her in-laws. As she had reminded her husband, upon learning of Arthur's death, Elizabeth was pregnant again with what was hoped to be another prince. The king and queen were also focussed on their eldest daughter's upcoming marriage to the king of Scotland, James IV, and all their attention was on preparations for her household.

On 2 February 1502, the queen gave birth whilst staying in the Tower of London. The Tower at this time did not have quite the fearsome reputation it would have in the future and was in fact still used as a royal residence, but as there are no records of Elizabeth preparing to take to her chamber at this time we are left with the conclusion she went into labour prematurely. The new baby was not the hoped for prince either but another princess who they named Katherine, possibly after Catherine, but equally possibly after Elizabeth's sister to whom she was close. Just days after the birth of her last child, tragedy was to strike the royal family again as on 11 February, her thirty-seventh birthday, Elizabeth of York suddenly passed away from childbed fever; a double blow followed with the death of the infant princess just a few days after her mother.[9]

Elizabeth's death devastated her family and there was a marked change in the behaviour of her husband afterwards. Whilst he had always been careful with money, it was after Elizabeth's death that his reputation for miserliness really started to spread and it would have a direct impact on Catherine herself. Elizabeth's loss also impacted Catherine personally as she lost a figure who could have been a mentor and surrogate mother to her; she had certainly been one of the few people to think of Catherine after Arthur's death.

However, Elizabeth's death had the potential to impact Catherine in another perhaps unforeseen way. As a widower and with only one son, Henry was now looking for a new wife. This is not to be taken as a comment on his relationship with Elizabeth but as dynastic need, and his eye briefly fell upon his widowed daughter-in-law before her mother shut down the whole idea. Isabella wrote that it was a 'very evil thing, one never before seen and the mere mention of which offends the ears …we would not for anything in the world that it should take place'.[10] Whilst a marriage to Henry would have instantly reinstated the marital alliance between Spain and England, there was no guarantee that Henry would have any more children with Catherine and, if he did, they would only be second to Prince Henry and his future children. In a more brutal train of thought, Catherine would likely only be queen for a handful of years before Henry's death and, whilst she may marry again, time and her youth would have been wasted. Isabella's firm refusal did have a positive effect as it led to the betrothal of Prince Henry to her daughter. A new treaty was signed on 23 June 1503 and the betrothal ceremony took place on 25 June at Salisbury House in London; Catherine wore white for the occasion.[11] The dispensation required to allow the marriage would not arrive in England until 1504 though both sides lobbied successive Popes for it. As the marriage was not going to take place sooner than 1505, the year Prince Henry turned 14, this was at the time more of a bureaucratic annoyance than anything else.

After their betrothal, Catherine was seen more frequently at court, though the couple were not allowed to spend much time together. It was another Tudor she would grow closer to – the Princess Mary, her youngest sister-in-law – who would become a lifelong friend and supporter. Throughout 1504, Catherine travelled with the court to Greenwich, Richmond, Westminster and Windsor – the trip to Windsor may have been classed as a short break for the king as he spent around twelve days hunting, with Catherine in attendance. Unfortunately, in August, Catherine fell ill with what was described as an 'ague and derangement of the stomach'.[12] She returned to Durham House to recuperate but she became sicker; sources describe her as suffering from a loss of appetite, chills and sweating and a cough, and it was not until the end of the month that she would be on the mend much to everyone's relief. Catherine may have become ill through stress as it was observed that there was trouble in her household. Money was tight, and it led to disagreements that became so bad that Catherine asked Henry to intervene but there was nothing he could do as her household were Spanish subjects and outside his jurisdiction, although he did discreetly aid her.

Whilst staying at Westminster Palace in November 1504, Catherine wrote to her parents complaining that she had not heard from them in so long. She wrote that her sister, Juana, had informed her of both of their parent's ill health. Ferdinand had suffered from a fever but Isabella had suffered from daily attacks of ague followed by fever that caused great concern to her husband; in Easter of 1504 he had been concerned enough to firmly insist Isabella retire temporarily and take some time to recuperate. Whilst this appeared to produce a brief respite for the queen it was not to last. Tragically, on the day Catherine was writing of her concern for them, Queen Isabella of Castile died aged 53.

Catherine did not receive the terrible news straight away as letters were still being sent by De Puebla addressed to both the king and queen on 5 December, but she must have known of her loss later in the month. Whilst a devastating personal blow to Catherine, it was a political one too. Ferdinand and Isabella's marriage had united Spain and they had been the most powerful monarchs of their time. Their realms were now split with her sister Juana inheriting Castile and Ferdinand remaining solely as King of Aragon. Catherine was now only

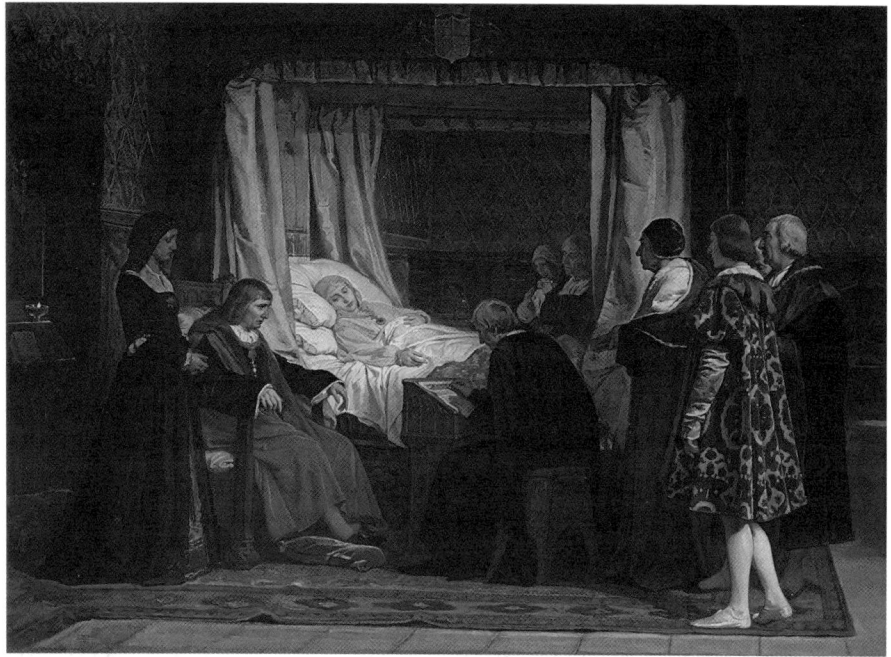

Queen Isabella the Catholic dictating her Will by Eduardo Rosales, c.1864. Isabella's loss was both personal and political for Catherine; it left her without a much-loved mother and one of the few people who was genuinely interested in her welfare for her own sake. Politically it left her as only a daughter of Aragon and devalued her in the marriage market. (*Public Domain image, via Wikimedia Commons*)

a daughter of the King of Aragon, a much smaller country, and she instantly became a lesser prize on the marriage market. Added to this was the trouble between Juana's husband and their father – both men wanted to rule Castile through Juana – and even Juana's own precarious health. Isabella, Ferdinand and Philip had had an uneasy relationship for several years prior to Isabella's death, the biggest problem being Philip's obviously pro-French policies. In her will, Isabella attempted to safeguard Castile by nominating Ferdinand to act for Juana until her eldest son came of age, if there was ever a reason she could not rule herself. Juana's health issues were mental not physical and whilst there does appear to have been a genuine medical issue, perhaps a breakdown, during Isabella's lifetime, there is some debate today as to how bad they became in the years after Isabella's death. Some historians have suggested that her issues were exaggerated to allow the men in her life to seize power and rule in her stead. Whatever the truth, there was going to be a power struggle for Castile and this was not lost on Henry VII who secretly commanded his son to break off his engagement to Catherine on 27 June 1505, just before his fourteenth birthday.[13] Henry now had an ace up his sleeve; publicly his son and Catherine

Philip the Fair and Juana of Aragon and Castile by the Master of Affligem. Left panel: *c*.1505–1506; right panel: *c*.1495–1506. Catherine was delighted to see her sister again but their time together was brief. (*Public Domain image, via Wikimedia Commons*)

were betrothed but privately and unbeknownst to Catherine the betrothal was broken and the prince could marry elsewhere.

Catherine's problems would only worsen. Despite her presence in England she found herself embroiled in the affairs of Castile and torn between her loyalty and love for her father and sister. Philip had written and sent ambassadors to Catherine and her duenna and Elvira Manuel encouraged her to write to Henry and propose a meeting between the two men so they could form an alliance. Manuel and her husband were supporters of Philip and were attempting to embroil Catherine in a plan to unseat her own father. It was only the actions of De Puebla that stopped the scheme in its tracks. He revealed Manuel's duplicity to Catherine, who angrily dismissed her from her household. On De Puebla's instructions, Catherine anxiously wrote to Henry begging him to 'value the interests of her father, the King of Spain, beyond those of any Prince in the world'.

By strange coincidence the meeting Catherine had been manipulated into suggesting did take place in January 1506. Sailing from Burgundy to claim Juana's throne, the couple were caught in a storm that forced them to seek shelter in England. Prince Henry was sent to welcome them, and upon meeting and spending time with the new King of Castile developed an admiration of Philip that never waned. His father used this stroke of luck to conclude a treaty that stipulated neither Philip or Henry would harbour each other's enemies and any fugitives or exiles found in their lands would be handed over. This meant Philip was required to hand over the 'White Rose' Edmund de la Pole, Duke of Suffolk, one of the last potential rivals for Henry's throne, who was imprisoned on his arrival back in England. The treaty also included a marriage alliance with Philip's sister and Catherine's sister-in-law, Margaret of Austria, for the king.

Catherine met Philip for the first time at Windsor where she performed a Spanish dance for him but the occasion became awkward when Philip rudely refused to dance with Catherine when she asked. On a happier note, she was able to greet and dine with her sister for the first time in ten years, followed by a short, supervised meeting where they talked for a while; Catherine would never see another of her siblings again.[14]

For Catherine personally, money was the major ongoing issue. Her dowry had never been completely paid and for that reason she was not entitled to her income as Arthur's widow and to save money Henry closed her household at Durham House and Catherine moved to live permanently at court. Henry made it quite clear to her that what he did for her he did out of charity and that he was under no obligation to provide for her at all. Catherine, acutely aware of how embarrassing her situation was, wrote multiple times to her father pleading for his help and to settle her dowry. One such letter survives in part and from what it does tell us, it is clear she was rather desperate at the time of writing.

> *[I cannot] speak more particularly, because I know not what will become of this letter, or if it will arrive at the hands of your Highness; but when Don Pedro de Ayala shall come, who is now with the King and Queen in the harbour, your*

Highness shall know all by ciphers. I have written many time to Your Highness, supplicating you to order a remedy for my extreme necessity, of which [letters] I never had an answer. Now I supplicate Your Highness, for the love of Our Lord, that you consider how I am your daughter, and that after HIM our Saviour I have no other good nor remedy, except in Your Highness; and how I am in debt in London, and this not for extravagant things, nor yet by relieving my own people, who greatly need it, but only for food; and how the King of England, my lord, will not cause them [the debts] to be satisfied, although I myself spoke to him, and all those of his Council, and that with tears; but he said that he is not obliged to give me anything, and that even the food he gives me is of his good will; because Your Highness has not kept promise with him in the money of my marriage portion. I told him that I believed that in time to come Your Highness would discharge it. He told me that that was yet to see, and that he did not know it. So that, my Lord, I am in the greatest trouble and anguish in the world. On the one part, seeing all my people that they are ready to asks alms; on the other, the debts which I have in London.

About my own person, I have nothing for chemises; wherefore, by Your Highness life, I have now sold some bracelets to get a dress of black velvet, for I was all but naked; for since I departed hence [from Spain] I have had nothing except two new dresses, fortill now, those I brought from thence have lasted me; although now I have got nothing but the dresses of brocade. On this account, I supplicate Your Highness to command to remedy this, and that as quickly as may be; for certainly I shall not be able to live in this manner. I likewise supplicate Your Highness to do me so great a favour as to send me a Franciscan Observant friar, who is a man of letters, for a confessor, because as I have written at other times to Your Highness, I do not understand the English language, nor how to speak it: and I have no confessor. And this should be, if Your Highness will so command it, very quickly; because you truly know the inconvenience of being without a confessor, especially now to me, who, for six months have been near death: but now, thanks to Our Lord, I am somewhat better, although not entirely well. This I supplicate Your Highness once again that it may be as soon as possible. Calderon, who brings this letter, has served me very well. He is now going to be married. I have not wherewith to recompense him I supplicate Your Highness to do me so great a favour as to command him to be paid there [in Spain] and have him recommended; for I have such care for him that any favour that Your Highness may do him I should receive as most signal.

Our Lord guard the life and most royal estate of Your Highness, and increase it as I desire. From Richmond, the 22nd April.

The humble servant of your Highness, who kisses your hands.
The Princess of Wales.[15]

Ferdinand received a firmer rebuke closer to home from Juan Lopez, the Trustee of Queen Isabella. Catherine was clearly not forgotten by those without a familial connection to her either:

> *Has done all in his power to remedy the great embarrassment of the Princess of Wales, as Monsieur Ferrer will write more circumstantially; but is afraid that the trustees will not be able to assist her effectually. They have nothing in their keeping but the two jewels of the Crown and a collar. The trustees do not think it advisable to send the jewels to England, where they would not be paid for according to their value. But it is a sad thing to hear of the necessity of the Princess, and not to help her. The trustees offer the two jewels and the collar to him, and ask him to send money to the Princess, who is not only the daughter of the late Queen, but also his child. The poverty of the Princess reflects dishonour on his, and on the late Queen's name. If she had been alive, she would not have suffered it, even if the Princess had not been her daughter. It is the duty of a King to succour a young Princess who is living in a foreign land without protection, and exposed to such dangers as the Princess of Wales. – Valladolid, 28th August.*[16]

Catherine's next problem, though she would maybe not realise until later, was the arrival of her new confessor in 1507. Fray Diego Fernandez was a Spanish friar dispatched to England by the Order of the Franciscan Friars Observant in Spain who quickly gained influence over Catherine's entire mind and her actions, and it caused her to make a series of missteps. Whilst nothing improper ever took place between them, the fact that the friar was able to gain such a hold over Catherine reinforces how difficult her circumstances were at this time. She had no money and had resorted to selling some of her plate to make ends meet, she was virtually friendless in a foreign land, her father and father-in-law appeared to be doing very little to aid her and were more focussed on blaming each other for her situation. She had lost friends she thought she could trust and her marriage to the prince was no closer to being celebrated. Her only source of comfort and solace was her confessor, who listened and sympathised with her. It appears Catherine also started selling more of her plate and jewels to buy items the friar said he required. He was so influential that he managed to shake her iron clad belief in her betrothal to Prince Henry. He convinced her that Henry himself had defaulted on the terms and that she need no longer abide by them herself or suffer more humiliation. Catherine was so convinced by his arguments she even wrote of them to her father, but he ignored her.

Their relationship developed to the point that Catherine would not do anything that would risk the friar's disapproval, and when he forbade her to travel to Richmond with Princess Mary in March 1509 following an illness, she acquiesced, and Mary departed alone. No provisions had been put in place for her to remain at their current house and when word reached the king, he was furious and refused to speak to her for around three weeks. Her actions were not just insulting to him but inconvenient to the court.¹⁷

Before this, however, Ferdinand did finally do something to help his beleaguered daughter. In 1507, in an extraordinary move, Ferdinand created his daughter Ambassador to England. This position immediately enhanced Catherine's status and brought a new degree of respect and recognition, ensuring she could now not be ignored at Henry's court. It also provided her with a first-hand education in the politics of England and Europe, Catherine took to her new appointment like a duck to water. She was issued her own diplomatic cipher and learned to read and write in code and was now able to deal with her father-in-law on a more equal footing.¹⁸ She grew in confidence, using flattery and compliments to placate him, but would even dispute with him on occasion. She provided advice to her father, aiding him in his goals and followed his commands.

Mary Tudor drawn whilst she was queen of France, unknown artist. c.1514–15. Mary was King Henry VII and Queen Elizabeth of York's youngest surviving daughter. (*Public Domain image, via Wikimedia Commons*)

A significant moment occurred for her when Henry became interested in marrying Queen Juana. Philip had died in September 1506, leaving the queen of Castile a widow, and it is from this time that a disturbing story has come down to us about Juana's behaviour. It is said she refused to allow her husband's burial and whilst the cortege made its way to his final resting place in Granada, she would repeatedly open the coffin and kiss the corpse and refused to allow any other woman nearby. The stories surrounding Philip's corpse are not backed up by first-hand accounts and it appears her travelling with his funeral cortege has been twisted. Whilst Juana did insist on his burial place in Granada, this was most likely a decision made from a dynastic point of view. Philip himself had specifically requested to be buried there; he had been king of Spain and their children would inherit the throne from her. She had inherited the throne from her own mother who was also laid to rest in Granada and Granada had itself become the symbol of Christian Spain.

Whether Catherine was aware of all the sordid stories spreading about her sister we don't know, but she was informed that Juana was too grief-stricken to consider remarriage just yet, but Ferdinand promised to bring her around to the idea. Henry himself had heard tales of her mental state but claimed not to care as she was beautiful and clearly capable of producing children. Henry stated he had been impressed by Juana when he had met her and Catherine, despite having first-hand experience of Henrys character, wrote to her sister singing Henry's praises to encourage the match – not an action she would have taken if she knew her sister to be unwell or insane. For Catherine, Juana's marriage to Henry would hopefully bring about her own long delayed marriage and she would use any available ploy, even leaving out a true character description of Henry to her sister, to achieve it. She met with De Puebla and his colleague, Gutierre Gomez de Fuensalida, who had been sent by her parents to keep an eye on the former in 1499 but who later returned as an ambassador himself. They wrote to Ferdinand and her mother's old confessor, Cardinal Ximinez de Cisneros, to try and bring about the match whilst keeping Henry up to date and interested in the progression of the marriage discussions. Catherine had to tread a very fine line, urging a course she believed in but committing to nothing, using fair and diplomatic words and speeches to keep communications open, managing a sometimes difficult man in her father-in-law who had treated her less than respectfully and continuing to work towards her own marriage. Whilst Henry and Juana would never marry, Catherine herself was not blamed and the experience she gained from this time would serve her well in the future.[19]

In 1508, Ferdinand finally made the decision to settle Catherine's outstanding dowry and he announced the remaining difference would be paid in cash instead of using Catherine's plate. Whilst this seemed a step in the right direction for Catherine, there was still no guarantee this would lead to her marriage. In fact she was aware of discussions taking place for a match between Prince Henry and Eleanor of Austria, Catherine's niece, and she was aware that her friend Mary was betrothed to Eleanor's brother Charles, the future Holy Roman Emperor. Where did that leave her?

Chapter 4

Queen of England

On 21 April 1509, Henry VII died at Richmond Palace aged 52. Despite his unpopularity, he left England in a much better state than he found it. Her reputation and prestige abroad had improved, the country was solvent and perhaps most importantly, Henry was the first king of England in over eighty years to pass on his throne peacefully to his heir. Prince Henry, now King Henry VIII, was just 17 but no regency ever appears to have been seriously suggested, although his grandmother did supervise the transition of power and helped with preparations for his coronation.

The death of the old king was not announced straight way and it is likely Catherine herself found out about the death of her father-in-law

Catherine's personal badge.
(*Public Domain image, via Wikimedia Commons*)

on 24 April when it was announced to the court. She was included in the list of mourners and issued with black cloth for her mourning attire, that was also provided for eight members of her household – two ladies, four gentlewomen and two chamberers. Interestingly, the accounts show payments for saddlery and livery for her servants against the internment, implying that Catherine was expected to attend the funeral and the procession. This was an unusual step for royalty at this time, but more than likely refers to her role as Ambassador to England; ambassadors were expected to attend the funerals of royalty.[1]

Earlier that month, Ferdinand instructed his new ambassador, Miguel Perez Almazan, to try once more to bring about the marriage of Catherine and Henry, even making it a condition of the future marriage of Princess Mary and Prince Charles. If he was unable to, he was to make arrangements for Catherine's return to Spain where a new marriage would be decided for her. Upon the death of Henry VII, however, everything changed.

Henry VIII decided he would honour his previous betrothal to Catherine and instructed his councillors to make the necessary arrangements; it appears he had no interest in any other woman as his wife and queen. Negotiations began before the dead king was even interred, and on 3 May a delegation that included the Lord Privy Seal, Richard Foxe, who was also Bishop of Winchester, officially visited Ambassador Fuensalida in his lodgings to conclude the arrangements. Foxe advised the ambassador that the king wanted to marry Catherine and his council was currently in favour of the match, so if Ferdinand also still wanted the marriage to proceed, any negotiations should be concluded as soon as possible. Just five days later an agreement was made. For Catherine, seven long years of uncertainty and poverty were now over, and she stood vindicated in her belief and cause – she was finally to marry her prince.

On 11 June 1509, Henry and Catherine were finally married in a quiet ceremony held

King Henry VIII attributed to Meynnart Wewyck, *c.*1509. Henry's accession was greeted with widespread celebration and shortly after he decided to honour his betrothal to Catherine; the two were married on 11 June 1509. (*Public Domain image, via Wikimedia Commons*)

The Palace of Placentia, better known as Greenwich Palace, *c.* seventeenth century. Henry VIII and Catherine were quietly married here. (*Public Domain image, via Wikimedia Commons*)

at Greenwich Palace. Two of the witnesses were Lord Steward Shrewsbury and the Groom of the Privy Chamber, William Thomas. This was a stark contrast to Catherine's first wedding, but as it came so soon after the late king's death it was necessary. In fact none of Henry's marriage ceremonies would be public affairs, it would be the celebrations after them that would provide the spectacle, although it can be assumed that both the bride and groom will have been magnificently dressed.

There was one note of discord in this otherwise happy occasion, though it is not clear if Catherine was aware of it. Prior to their marriage, the Archbishop of Canterbury, William Warham, expressed his doubts on the legality of their future union given Catherine's previous marriage to Henry's brother, but he was either persuaded or let it go as it was he who provided the marriage licence for the ceremony.² Interestingly, Ambassador Fuensalida learned from one of his sources that Henry himself had scruples of conscience and was unsure if he should, or could, marry Catherine. Either this was a rumour, a ploy by a councillor, or Henry never in fact said it, as it would be over twenty years before he would mention it publicly.³

William Warham, Archbishop of Canterbury, by Hans Holbein the younger, c.1528. (*Public Domain image, via Wikimedia Commons*)

Just two weeks later, Henry and Catherine made a state entry into London. This was of course not the first time Catherine had been greeted by Londoners, but this time circumstances were different. Now she was entering as the wife of the king and on her way to their coronation. Once again London did not disappoint – the streets were cleaned and sanded, barriers erected to control the crowds, tapestries, silks and cloth of gold and arras hung from the railings and windows and tailors found themselves working night and day to make the robes and costumes that would be needed by officials for the various stages of the celebration. The last joint coronation to take place in England was that of Richard III and his queen, Anne Neville, in 1483 and its possible it may have acted as a blueprint for Henry and Catherine's. Though given the way Richard had come to the throne and the Tudor dynasty's own personal history with him,

The Tower of London. (*Author's Collection*)

it is almost certain this was not mentioned if this was the case. By 23 June, everything was ready.

At around four in the afternoon, Henry and Catherine left the Tower of London and progressed through Gracechurch Street, Cornhill and Cheapside. Henry rode a great horse draped in cloth of gold fabric beneath a gold Canopy of Estate. He was magnificently dressed in a robe of red velvet trimmed with ermine and a golden coat studded with precious stones; the ensemble was finished with a gold collar studded with jewels. He was escorted by the Duke of Buckingham in his role as Constable of England and the Knights of the Bath, passing bishops and priests whose role it was to cense the new king and queen. The procession included the heralds and the gentleman and courtiers.[4]

At a distance, Catherine followed her husband with an equally impressive escort including many of the people who had stood by her during the difficult years prior. She wore a gown of exquisitely embroidered white satin with 'a rich mantle of gold tissue', and her litter and horses (also white) were decorated in white cloth of gold fabric. Like previous queen consorts, she wore her red-gold hair loose 'hangyng donne to her backe, of a very great length, bewetefull and goodly to behold' as a symbol of purity and a gold and pearl coronet.[5] Her ladies were dressed in cloth of silver and gold, velvet and ermine and rode on horseback or in chariots with her.

As appears to have become a tradition in Catherine's family, the day was slightly spoiled by a turn of the weather. A sudden shower forced Catherine to temporarily halt the procession and take cover under the awning of a draper's stall. Once it passed, they immediately continued, allowing nothing to spoil this most special of days.

Westminster Abbey. Henry and Catherine were jointly crowned king and queen of England in this historic building. (*Author's Collection*)

At Cheapside, the royal couple were greeted by the Mayor of London and the guildsman of the city, whilst Catherine was also greeted with virgins dressed in white holding lighted tapers. They continued the procession to their destination at Westminster Palace, where they lodged for the night.[6] It was likely a night of anticipation for both Henry and Catherine; did they get much rest? Were they worried about the duty that was about to be invested in them? Were they excited? Likely they were feeling all sorts of emotions. Catherine had already proven that she could and would bear trying circumstances and the crown was both a burden and an honour, but she never shied away from a challenge, nor would she in future. Out of the two, Catherine was the readiest for the crown and she would need to help her husband going forward, a duty she was happy to undertake.

At eight o clock the next morning, Henry and Catherine, dressed in matching crimson robes, processed to Westminster Abbey along a striped ray cloth strewn with flowers, to two thrones awaiting them on a platform before the altar. The coronation ceremony was performed by the Archbishop of Canterbury who administered the oath to Henry then anointed him with holy oil. He reverently handed Henry the golden orb and sceptre and lastly placed the crown of St Edward the Confessor, used for all king's coronations, on his head. It was then Catherine's turn. She was also anointed on her head and breast and handed a golden sceptre, but instead of an orb was given an ivory rod with a dove on top, to represent equity and mercy, and a ring was placed on the fourth finger of her right hand symbolising her marriage to her England. She was crowned with a gold coronet set with sapphires, rubies and pearls.[7]

Catherine was now the crowned and anointed queen of England, and no one could dispute her title. She had finally accomplished the task her parents had entrusted to her: England and Spain were allies; the alliance was sealed by marriage, though not the one everyone had planned for; and her troubles were

Woodcut depicting the coronation of King Henry VIII and Catherine of Aragon in 1509, by an unknown artist, *c.* sixteenth century. (*Public Domain image, via Wikimedia Commons*)

at an end. Now her future was bright and settled and she could look forward to many years as England's queen and the mother of heirs to the throne.

Upon exiting the Abbey, the new king and queen greeted their subjects, who responded with rapturous cheers and applause as they walked in procession to Westminster Hall where a great feast of 'plentifull abundance …whiche was sumptuous, with many subtelties, strange devices …and many deintie dishes' awaited them. The Duke of Buckingham rode into the hall on a mount covered in gold fabric to announce the courses, whilst Sir John Dimmock also rode into the hall and demanded to know whether there was any person present who challenged the right of Henry as inheritor of the realm. This was not as dramatic as it sounded, but a choreographed tradition at coronations for the king's champion to ride in and demand this of the guests. Nobody disputed the king's claim and Henry sent his champion a gold cup to drink from as the heralds proclaimed his right. Once the feast was finished, dishes of wafers were served and the Mayor served the king with hippocras wine before everyone departed.

Sir Thomas More by Hans Holbein the Younger, *c*.1527. More wrote verses celebrating Henry and Catherine's marriage and coronation but years later he would find himself in opposition to the king for siding with the queen. (*Public Domain image, via Wikimedia Commons*)

Over the next few days, the celebrations continued with tournaments and jousting. Henry and Catherine observed the celebrations from a newly constructed 'faire house' that provided shelter. Decorated with tapestries and rich cloth, its companion was a castle decorated with a vine of gold leaves and grapes wound round and erected over a fountain which held gargoyles that produced red and white wine from their mouths. It was also gilded with roses and pomegranates (Henry and Catherine's personal symbols), the new king and queen's initials and the Tudor colours of green and white. Catherine had chosen the pomegranate as her symbol for its associations: it was a widely recognised symbol of fertility and Catherine hoped to be the mother of many sons and daughters. It was also a symbol of her homeland; Isabella and Ferdinand had incorporated the pomegranate into their own royal arms following the surrender of Granada where it had been a part of the province's heraldry and a universally recognised emblem. Granada in Spanish also translates to pomegranate.

One of the pageants involved some young gallants presented to Henry by the Goddess of Widom who wished to do 'feats of arms for the love of the ladies' with the Knights of Diana presented to Catherine, representing love. The 'tournament' only came to an end because night was falling.[8]

A young lawyer named Thomas More, who had witnessed both Catherine's arrival in England and her coronation, wrote verses for the occasion and the resulting text will have pleased them both:

This lady, prince, vowed to you for many years, through
a long time of waiting remained alone for love of you.
Neither her own sister nor her native land could win her
from her way; neither her mother nor her father
could dissuade her.

In her you have as wife one whom your people have
Been happy to see sharing your power,
One for whom the powers above care so much that they
Distinguish her and honour her by marriage with you.

In her expression, in her countenance, there is a remarkable
Beauty unique appropriate for one so great and good.

It was you, none other, whom she preferred to her
mother, sister, native land, and beloved father.

This blessed lady has joined in lasting alliance two
Nations, each of them powerful.

She is descended from great kings, to be sure; and she
will be the mother of kings as great as her ancestors.

Until now one anchor has protected your ship of state-
A strong one, yet only one
But your queen, fruitful in male offspring, will render it
On all sides stable and everlasting.

Great advantage is yours because of her, and similarly is hers because of you.

There has been no other woman, surely, worthy to have
You as husband, nor any other man worthy to have her as wife.[9]

If it was at all possible, the celebrations doubled upon Henry's 18th birthday, on 28 June 1509. There was hunting and another pageant where the returning gallants of Henry and Catherine requested permission to do battle again, but when love and wisdom were unable to defeat each other Henry rewarded them all. Tragedy marred the celebrations slightly with the death of Margaret Beaufort the day after Henry's birthday, but it was not allowed to ruin the festivities. It was a poignant but clean break with the past. Both Henry and Catherine were now the only senior royal figures in England, and they could set the tone and course to come.

A total of £1536 16s 2d was spent on Catherine's coronation preparations; the amount was only slightly surpassed by her husband who spent £1749 8s 4d. They were equal and united in their celebrations and both wanted to make a good impression and a truly memorable spectacle for one of the most important moments of their reigns. Whilst at Greenwich Palace, Catherine wrote to her father of her happiness and love for her husband. In a rare instance for Ferdinand, he had been taken aback by the speed of the turnaround of Catherine's fortunes in England and had held public celebrations of his own in which he had even taken part to mark her marriage and accession.[10]

In an excerpt from a letter dated 29 July, Catherine wrote:

And it is the greatest favour that your highness can do me and most conformed to my will, since I know that in this life I have no other good except that of being your daughter; although [by] your highness so well married, that more cannot be said, except that it is the work of those hands of your highness which I kiss for signal a favour.

As to the king my lord, amongst the reasons that oblige me to love him much more than myself, the one most strong, although he is my husband, is his being the so true son of your highness, with desire of greater obedience and love to serve you than ever son had to his father. I have performed the office of Ambassador as your highness sent to command, and as was known by the king my lord, who is, and places himself entirely, in the hands of your highness, as of so entire a father and lord. And your highness may believe me, that he is such in keeping obedience to your highness as could never have been thought, from which Increase in infinite pleasure as much as reason requires.

The news from here is that those kingdoms of your highness are in great peace, and entertain much love toward the king my lord and to me. His highness and I are very hearty to the service of your highness. Our time is ever passed in continual feasts. I supplicate your highness, as to the favour which you have always bestowed upon me, in which you have shown me the greatest favour, henceforth to bestow it on me, by showing that you esteem the king my lord and me as your true children.

She finished with a postscript:

> *I supplicate you highness to do me so signal a favour as to send to the king my lord three horses – one a jennet, and the other from Naples, and the other a Sicilian; because he desires them much, and has asked me to beg your highness for them: in which I shall receive a great favour from your highness; and also to command them to be sent by the first messenger that comes here.*[11]

Catherine of Aragon's signature as queen. (*Public Domain image, via Wikimedia Commons*)

Chapter 5

Good Queen Catherine

Following their coronation, a significant act of Henry's reign took place in July and August 1509: the conviction of Richard Empson and Edmund Dudley for treason. Empson and Dudley had been Henry VII's tax collectors and they had been rather skilled at their job, much to the annoyance of practically the whole kingdom. So when Henry had them arrested and charged with treason, no one was sorry to see them go. But it was a very early, and missed, warning of things to come. Empson and Dudley had done nothing wrong and, in fact, had only done exactly what their master, the dead king, had commanded of them. However, their unpopularity and Henry VII's death left them vulnerable. It was an easy diplomatic and public relations coup for his successor to have them tried and executed; it increased Henry's already large popularity with his subjects but it was also a stark warning of how disposable people could become to Henry. Did anyone realise this at the time? Did Catherine? Whilst everything was currently going well for her, she had suffered under one king's rule already and knew how easily fortune could turn to disaster. Presently she was enjoying her triumph, but she had become an experienced diplomat in recent years, and it is probable that she was aware that the two men had not committed treason. But perhaps she had suffered from their money-making schemes as well, and felt that although they hadn't committed treason, they had certainly committed a moral crime.

More happily for Catherine, Margaret Pole was given an annuity of £100 a year. Margaret had struggled since the death of her husband in 1504, but now that Catherine was queen she remembered her friend from Ludlow and was able to assist her. Henry was not as suspicious of his

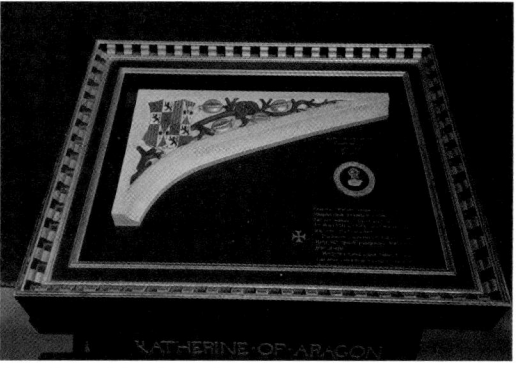

A replica of the decor Catherine would have been familiar with in the palaces; her personal symbol of the pomegranate would have been particularly prominent. (*Author's collection*)

Yorkist relatives (yet) as his father had been, but he had had very little to do with Margaret as she had been more closely associated with his brother's household. It is likely that Catherine used her own good fortune to intercede for her old friend. She appointed her as one of her principal attendants during her coronation and she was given livery clothing and lodged at the king's expense in London.[1]

But whilst Catherine had been educated to be a queen, she now had to apply her knowledge practically. Her education and recent experiences had taught her the skills she needed to survive in the political world, but as the queen of England she had many more duties and responsibilities. Firstly, she had to organise her household and for that she would need to manage her lands. She was entitled to her lands (or jointure) through her marriage, and they would bring in the revenue needed to maintain her household and her own obligations. Whilst she would never need to be 'hands on', she did need to ensure her lands and properties were well maintained and able to generate revenue for her expenses. Catherine received lands that totalled £4129, a large amount at the time, but an amount that could quickly disappear.[2]

Catherine of Aragon as the Magdalene by Michael Sittow, c.1515–16. (*Public Domain image, via Wikimedia Commons*)

As queen, Catherine was expected to maintain a certain image and for that she needed to be dressed splendidly, with the best fabrics and jewels, and she needed to pay embroiderers and goldsmiths to provide them for her. Whilst in private she preferred simpler clothes like her mother, in public she appeared magnificently dressed as the queen she was.

Proof of how richly Henry and Catherine dressed was confirmed in January 2023 when a pendant and chain was unearthed in Warwickshire. Made of gold and enamel and shaped like a heart, it was decorated with the Tudor rose and a pomegranate alongside the initial's H and K. Whilst there is no direct proof yet that the necklace belonged to Henry or Catherine, the quality and materials used indicate it could only be owned by someone of the higher nobility.[3]

Catherine introduced embroidery known as black work to England – the most notable example can be found in Hans Holbein's later portrait of her successor, Jane Seymour. Another innovation she introduced was the Farthingale

Nottingham High School Charter, *c.*1512. The outer decoration consists of Tudor roses and pomegranates, Henry and Catherine's personal symbols. (*Public Domain image, via Wikimedia Commons*)

Catherine's coat of arms as queen of England. (*Author's collection*)

or 'vardinagale', named for the Spanish word 'verdugos' after the supple green twigs used to create the hoops that made the distinctive shape of the skirt. The Farthingale would remain popular for centuries to come. Those who credit Catherine's successor, Anne Boleyn, for her keen sense of fashion and trendsetting often don't realise that Catherine was doing the same two decades earlier.

Catherine provided food and livery for some members of her household and also her kitchens, stables and bargemen who fed her and ensured she could travel around her kingdom. She needed money for charitable purposes: to give alms to the poor and make offerings in church or when she went on pilgrimage. She would also need money for personal gifts and expenses and as a queen she was expected to be generous.[4]

Maria with the Child by Michael Sittow c.1515. It is believed Catherine was the model for this portrait. (*Public Domain image, via Wikimedia Commons*)

In August 1509, Henry and Catherine set off on the first progress of their reign, travelling from Woking to Farnham, Wanstead and Hanworth before finishing at Greenwich Palace in October. A royal progress was a vital part of a monarch's rule that gave their usually more distant subjects the opportunity to see and be impressed and inspired by their king and queen, and hopefully ensure their people's continued loyalty and goodwill. On the other hand, a progress was an expensive and logistical nightmare for all involved as the king and queen could not travel lightly and residences had to be found to support the court along the journey and these were not always palaces. To save the royal household money, favoured courtiers often acted as hosts, sometimes to their detriment. But in Henry and Catherine's defence, they were not ungrateful guests and were acutely aware of the cost and effort involved, rewarding their hosts with gifts or signs of favour including patronage and advancement.

Catherine who had been constantly on the move with her own mother's court since she was a baby would likely have found this first English progress a rather simpler affair as it was based around the outskirts of London. For many years she had been used to travelling larger distances but she was able to put the skills she had picked up by her mother's side into practice.

Crown of King Henry VIII with the initials H and K for Henry and Catherine on one side. (*CNG, Wikimedia, CC 2.5. Public Domain image, via Wikimedia Commons*)

Catherine knew that to inspire loyalty she had to be seen and interact with her subjects. A progress provided the opportunity for them to make entrances into smaller cities and towns and travel in procession through them. Almost like a mini coronation procession, they would be greeted with pageants and provided with gifts from the local dignitaries and, perhaps most importantly for Catherine, she was able to visit local shrines, something that would become a source of enjoyment and comfort for her in the years to come. Catherine often went one step further – she would send her own agents ahead to enquire if anyone needed aid or support in the place she was about to visit or if anyone required an audience or simply wished to speak to her.

It was not all work and no play; time was set aside for amusements too. Catherine was a keen hunter who accompanied her hunt-obsessed spouse on many an occasion. She also enjoyed riding, hawking and birding alongside music and dancing, which were other passions of Henry's. They were a perfectly matched couple.

In December, the couple celebrated their first Christmas together at Richmond Palace where Henry spent nearly an entire year's revenue on the season. In 2017, the National Archives revealed that a document in the Royal Chamber Expenses Book showed that Henry spent the equivalent of £13.5 million on pageants, gifts, food and entertainment; the revenue for the same year was £16.5 million.[5] Catherine received an unusual surprise when twelve men dressed as Robin Hood and his Merry Men burst into her chamber unannounced, with musicians who quickly struck up a tune and led her and her ladies in a dance. Robin Hood was revealed to be a disguised Henry.[6] In Tudor times gifts were not exchanged until New Year's Day and Catherine's gift from Henry was a beautifully decorated missal – a book containing the texts used in the Catholic Mass throughout the year.

One of Catherine's first big tests as queen came via diplomacy and war. Her father launched a crusade against the Moors in Africa in 1511 and Henry wanted to be a part of it. Henry appears to have developed a hero worship of Ferdinand; whether this is down to his knowledge of Ferdinand and Isabella's victories, Catherines influence or perhaps both is unclear. Henry dispatched Thomas, Lord Darcy, as Admiral of his Fleet in March 1511 and wanted to go himself, but later in May sent 1000 archers to assist his father-in-law instead. Later the same month he signed a new treaty with Ferdinand, acknowledging the treaties of peace previously made between Ferdinand and Isabella and his father, desiring their continuance as 'the sovereigns who, by the marriage of Queen Catherine with the King of England, have become so nearly related'. Henry was firmly for Spain, and it delighted Catherine to see her home and adopted countries continue to be so closely allied.

However, both Catherine and Henry were being duped by her father. Whilst Ferdinand may have wanted to fight the Moors, his more immediate aim was to recover lands in Navarre from the French and he would use anyone and anything to achieve his goal. When Darcy had previously arrived in Spain, Ferdinand was not there to meet him and when the Admiral wrote and asked for instructions, Ferdinand replied that he and his men were to return to England. Ferdinand placated a peeved Henry by promising the opportunity to reclaim Aquitaine, once a part of the English Plantagenet empire. Pope Julius II, who was currently having his own difficulties with the French, wrote promising that in the event of French defeat, all Louis XII's realms and titles would be transferred to Henry, an even more glorious proposition in Henry's eyes.

This time, Henry committed 6000 men to Spain under a different Admiral, Sir Edward Howard, who would meet with Ferdinand in the north-east and cross the border into France with him. This time the results were even worse and humiliating for Henry. Ferdinand was again a no show, supplies began to run out, discipline broke down and quarrels broke out between Howard and Sir Thomas Grey, the man who Henry had dispatched with an additional 12,000 men for the cause. Both men had very different ideas on what to do in the trying circumstances they found themselves in. Howard wanted to stay and see the course Henry commanded through to the end but Grey, perhaps more realistically aware of their unenviable position, sided with the men who wanted to abandon the scheme all together. Howard was overruled and the English returned home. Henry's commands that they should stay arrived too late as the men had already set sail for England.

Ferdinand, with no hint of irony, immediately wrote complaining to Henry about his men's actions, claiming that the debacle was all Grey's fault and that the Spanish troops had been waiting in the Pyrenees to 'render the passage of the mountains safe' and guard their rear. He continued that because of Grey, an easy victory had been lost, and that he was quite frankly astonished at the reports he was receiving that the English had neither the resources nor the energy for the fight. Ferdinand then had the nerve to accuse the English of duplicity, stating he had heard rumours that an accord had been reached with the French and that was why the English lacked the stomach for a fight.[7]

The whole debacle put Catherine in a very tight spot between the two most important men in her life. Ferdinand dispatched his chief paymaster, Martin de Muxica, to communicate with Henry directly and wrote to Catherine stating that Muxica had something to say on his behalf and that he had commanded him to communicate it to her as well and she was to give him credence with her husband. When Muxica attempted to meet with Catherine before Henry, she wisely advised him that this was improper and that he must meet formerly with the king her husband first. She did discreetly write to him, advising Muxica that Henry was aware of everything that had gone on and how angry he was.

It later came out that Grey had been attempting to arrange a marriage between himself and the daughter of the late king of Navarre,[8] an action that enabled Catherine to champion the view of the injured Spanish and her father. Whilst this was later proven untrue, Catherine at this time believed it was and she used her influence to mediate with her countryman and advise her husband. She was able to steer her way through a very trying set of political and personal circumstances without attracting comments of favouritism and bias, accusations that had partially been responsible for the hatred aimed at one of her predecessors, Margaret of Anjou.

Soon after it was summer and Henry and Catherine left on progress again, this time visiting Northampton, Leicester Abbey, Coventry, Warwick and Nottingham. By November 1511, Henry and Ferdinand had clearly patched up their differences and signed the Treaty of Westminster, a pact that was designed to offset the growing power of France and Navarre. Henry did learn from this experience and would never again be as gullible as to trust everything Ferdinand said, but his relationship with Catherine was unchanged. He still seemed very much in love with her and stood by what he had written to Ferdinand soon after their marriage that 'The bond between them is now so strict that all their interests are common, and the love he bears to Katharine is such, that if he were still free he would choose her in preference to all others'.[9]

Three years into their marriage in 1512, a Spanish delegate noted that Henry 'treated her with care and affection' and was 'amazed at the great love the King

A portion of the Motet Celeste beneficium from a choir book for Henry VIII and Catherine of Aragon. (*Public Domain image, via Wikimedia Commons*)

professed towards the Queen' as he kissed and embraced her in public. Perhaps more importantly he still trusted her implicitly and when he made the decision to lead the next army into France himself it was Catherine he chose to be regent of England in his absence.[10]

Both Henry and Catherine were equally keen on war with France. Catherine herself approached the Venetian Ambassador to enquire about hiring Italian ships for the purpose and it was the same ambassador who succinctly wrote 'the King was bent on war, the council opposes it, and the Queen wills it'.[11] Whilst it may seem strange for two such well-regarded Catholics to be so keen on war, we must consider the influence and reasons for it. Catherine's parents had fought many a war, firstly to establish her mother's right to throne and then to reconquer the Moorish lands for Christianity – in their eyes both equal and worthy causes. Henry's cause had a religious overtone too as by this point the Pope had excommunicated Louis XII for trying to oust him. An excommunicated king was dangerously exposed, as Henry would find to his own cost in later years, as he could not rely on support from his fellow Catholic monarchs as they would not risk excommunication themselves, a reminder of how important and powerful God and the Church were in Tudor England.

By June 1513, Henry's expedition was ready to depart but he had one final duty to perform. On 11 June, Catherine was made Regent and Governess of England, Wales and Ireland. Catherine's role in Henry's absence would be to primarily defend the kingdom, but she would also be acting as support for her campaigning husband. Catherine was given the power to appoint sheriffs and issue warrants under her own seal, give assent to Church elections and issue commissions of muster. She was also able to make grants of land and if necessary convoke Parliament. The Treasurer was instructed to pay any sums of money ordered by the queen that she felt was necessary in defence of the kingdom.

Henry was to depart for France from Dover Castle, and he travelled with Catherine from Greenwich in a slow procession through Kent, stopping at Canterbury Cathedral where they both made offerings to the shrine of St Thomas Becket. Henry said goodbye to Catherine and England on 29 June, arriving in Calais later that evening. Catherine, as a loving and supportive wife, tried to keep in regular contact with her absent husband but Henry's loathing of writing was evident here and it was his almoner, Thomas Wolsey, who allayed Catherine's fears and concerns and acted as go between for the spouses. We are without Wolsey's responses, but two of Catherine's letters to him survive from this time. Both were written at Richmond Palace. The first letter is dated 26 July:

> *Maister Almoner, thinking that the kings departing from Calais shall cause that I shall not so often hear from his Grace for the great business in his journey that every day he shall have, I send now my servant to bring me word of the King, and he shall tarry there til another cometh, and this way I shall hear every week from thence and so I pray you to take the pains with every of my messengers to write to me of the kings health, and what he intendeth to do, for when you be so near our enemies I shall never be in rest til I see often letters from you; and doing this you shall give me cause to thank you, and I shall know that the mind that you have had ever to me continues still as my trust always has been. The brief that the Pope sent to the King I was very glad to see, and I shall be more to hear that he is the means either to make an honourable peace for the King, or else help on his part as much as she can, knowing that all the business that the King hath was first the business of the Church, and with this and the emperor together I trust to God that the King shall come home shortly with as great a victory as any Prince in the world, and this I pray God send him without need of any other Prince.*

Interestingly this letter is not entirely focussed on the war in France. In the second paragraph, Catherine refers to a lady formerly in her service who she doesn't believe is fit for high service. It is a little unclear what the woman in question had done to offend Catherine, but it appears to have been related to her aforementioned marriage; it's possible she married unsuitably or without Catherine's permission, which as she served in Catherine's household she was required to obtain. It has also been suggested that the lady may have gossiped about Catherine and her confessor's activities during her widowhood and the one thing Catherine could never forgive was disloyalty. This letter gives a rare glimpse into the multiple roles that both Wolsey and Catherine were trying to juggle; just because they were at war doesn't mean that ordinary business could be suspended:

Mr Almoner, touching Frances de Cassery's, matter, I thank you for your labour therein; true it is she was my women before she was married, but now since she cast herself away I have no more charge of her, For very pity to see her lost I prayed you in Canterbury to find the means to send her home to her country. Now you think that with my letter for recommendation to the Duchess of Savoy, she shall be content to take her into her service. This Mr Almoner is not meet for her, for she is so perilous a woman that it shall be dangerous to put her in a strange house. And you will do so much for to make her go hence by the way with the ambassador of the King my father, it should be to me a great pleasure, and with that you shall bind me to you more than I ever was.

She finishes by praising Henry's council and their diligent work on Henry's behalf. She also asks that Wolsey prompt Henry to acknowledge that she has spoken only praise of them:

From hence I have nothing to write to you. But everybody here is in good health, thanked be God, and the council very diligent in all things concerning the expedition of the Kings service. And you will do so much to pray the Kings grace to be so good lord as to write to them that he is informed by me so well … is done by them that he is very well content therewith and give them thanks for it, bidding them so to continue. And with this I make an end. At Richmond the 26th day of July.

Mr Almoner, after the writing of this letter my lord Admiral [Lord Howard] sent hither …which was taken with his ship and brought to him as the said …from Depe [Dieppe?] towards Flanders, and he hath shewn …things as be specified in a bill …a true man in his words. Inform the King …his pleasure shall be for I am assured the same sh.…

Katherine the Queen[12]

Good Queen Catherine 65

By the time of the second letter, Henry had captured the town of Therouanne and taken a prominent hostage, the Duke of Longueville, whom he sent to Catherine in England. He wanted her to keep him in her household, but Catherine was preparing for a war of her own, so the unfortunate duke was placed in honourable confinement in the Tower of London. It should be remembered that at this time the Tower didn't have quite the fearsome reputation it would later acquire, and whilst rarely used as a palace following the death of Queen Elizabeth, it was still a well-maintained royal residence. It was also a fortress and easily defendable should the worst happen.

Master almoner,

I received your letter by the post, whereby I understand of the coming hither of the duke, and the king is content that he shall be in my household. Touching this matter, I have spoken with the council to look and appoint what company shall be meet to attend upon him. Here is none that is good for it but my lord Mountjoy, who now goes to Calais as chief captain of the 500 men. And for this cause, and also that I am not so well accompanied as were convenient for his keeping here, it is thought to me and my council that it should be better the said duke be, as soon as he comes, conveyed to the Tower; especially the Scots being so busy as they now be, and I looking for my departing ever hour, it should be a great incumberence to me to have this prisoner here; seeing that, according to the kings mind, he must be conveyed to the Tower at my going forward. I pray you shew this to the king, and with the next messenger send me an answer of his pleasure.

Mr Almoner, I am sorry, knowing that I have been always so bound unto you, that now you shall think that I am miscontent without a cause, seeing that my servant asked of you no letter, nor brought you none from me. The cause was, that two days before I wrote unto you by Copinger, and at that time I had nothing further to write – and with my servants unwise demeanor I am nothing well content; for one of the greatest comforts that I have now is to hear, by your letters, of the kings health and of all your news. And so I pray you, Mr Almoner, to continue as hitherto you

Cardinal Thomas Wolsey by an unknown artist, c.1585–1596. (*Public Domain image, via Wikimedia Commons*)

have done: for I promise you that form henceforth you shall lack none of mine, and before this you have had many more, but I think your business scantly gives you leisure to read my letters. From hence I have nothing to write to you more than I am sure the council informs the king: praying God to send us as good luck against the Scots as the king had there.

At Richmond the 2nd day of September[13]

As Catherine hinted in her letter, trouble was brewing with Scotland. France and Scotland had maintained an alliance for hundreds of years, commonly referred to as the 'Auld Alliance' that was primarily based on acting as a deterrent to stop England from invading either country. In the event England did invade either country, then the other would invade England. The king of Scotland had threatened war when he learnt of Henry's plans in France, and throughout July and August 1513 tensions simmered along the Scottish and English border. By the end of August, the king of Scotland made his move: around 60,000 troops crossed the River Tweed and invaded England. The war in France was about to become a family affair as the king of Scotland was James IV, Henry and Catherine's own brother-in-law, who had married Henry's eldest sister, Margaret, in 1503.

Catherine and her council were prepared. Thomas Howard, 2nd Earl of Surrey, was made Lieutenant-General in the north and promptly set off to meet the invaders, recruiting more men along the way. A valued war veteran with experience and previous first-hand knowledge of the north from his time serving there during Henry VII's reign, as he approached Alnwick with around 26,000 men, he was joined by his sons, Thomas and Edmund, and their men. If the worst should happen, not all men and resources were concentrated in the North – Catherine and her council put in place two reserve armies. The first was commanded by Sir Thomas Lovell, who was ordered to recruit men from the Midlands, and the second would

A posthumous sketch of King James IV of Scotland by the sixteenth-century Wallonian artist, Jaques le Boucq. King James was Henry and Catherine's brother-in-law through his marriage to Henry's elder sister, Margaret. Catherine's army defeated his at the Battle of Flodden Field and James IV was killed in the battle. (*Public Domain image, via Wikimedia Commons*)

be led by Catherine herself and based in the south. Catherine travelled to Buckinghamshire where she reportedly made 'a splendid oration to the English captains'. She reminded them that 'the Lord smiled upon those who stood in defence of their own' and that 'English courage excelled that of all other nations'. Catherine had taken her mother's lessons to heart, and around this time it is recorded that the royal goldsmith, Robert Amadas, was paid for 'garnishing a head piece with a golden crown'.[14] As her mother had taught her, Catherine sounded and looked the part but it would be wrong to say she acted the part – she WAS the part. She firmly believed in her course of action and what her role in it needed to be and that she needed to inspire her men.

The battle between the English and Scottish armies would be a clear victory for one side and a resounding defeat for the other: England and Catherine won. The outcome of Flodden was eventually decided by terrain and the choice of weapons both sides used, but Catherine's abilities and organisational skills had played a huge part in their triumph. Whilst she was never anywhere near the field of battle, it was Catherine who organised the English defences, met with the council to discuss courses of action, and organised supplies and weapons. Nothing was done without her say so and any official documents were signed: 'Teste Katerina Angliae Regina ac Generali Rectrice Eiusdemi' or 'in witness of Catherine, Queen of England, and Governor-General of the same'.

Figures are unclear but is believed that the English lost around 1500 men at Flodden, whereas the Scottish lost at minimum 10,000 – but the total could have been as great as 17,000 men. Included in the fallen was the king of Scotland himself and a large proportion of the Scottish nobility. James IV's throne was inherited by Henry and Catherine's nephew, the new King James V, but he was not even 2 years old and until he reached his majority would require a regent. As a result, Scotland would not be able to cause problems for England for several years. The battle came to be known as the Battle of Flodden Field.[15]

Catherine wrote to Henry shortly after and we can hear the triumph and pride in her words:

Sir,

My Lord Howard hath sent me a letter open to your Grace, within one of mine, by the which you shall see at length the great Victory that our Lord hath sent your subjects in your absence; and for this cause there is no need herein to trouble your Grace with long writing, but, to my thinking, this battle hath been to your Grace and all your realm the greatest honor that could be, and more than you should win all the crown of France; thanked be God of it, and I am sure your Grace forgetteth not to do this, which shall be cause to send you many more such great victories, as I trust he shall do. My husband, for hastiness, with

Rougecross I could not send your Grace the piece of the King of Scots coat which John Glynn now brings. In this your Grace shall see how I keep my promise, sending you for your banners a king's coat. I thought to send himself unto you, but our Englishmens' hearts would not suffer it. It should have been better for him to have been in peace than have this reward. All that God sends is for the best.

My Lord of Surrey, my Henry, would fain know your pleasure in the burying of the King of Scots' body, for he has written to me so. With the next messenger your Grace's pleasure may be herein known. And with this I make an end, praying God to send you home shortly, for without this no joy here can be accomplished; and for the same I pray, and now go to Our Lady of Walsingham that I promised so long ago to see. At Woburn the 16th of September.

I send your Grace herein a bill found in a Scotsman's purse of such things as the French King sent to the said King of Scots to make war against you, beseeching you to send Mathew hither as soon as this messenger comes to bring me tidings from your Grace.

Your humble wife and true servant, Katharine.[16]

Catherine's victory and its implications for the future made Henry's insignificant in comparison. Given Henry's need to be admired and the centre of attention, it would not be unreasonable to suggest that he felt jealousy that his own wife had outshone him, though it doesn't appear to have ever come across in public. Whilst she was full of pride for her achievements, she was equally willing to share the credit, praising their people and remembering to thank God for his part in her success. She even regarded it as an honour to Henry. In her letters she always made sure to praise Henry's successes in France, and whilst this may look like mollycoddling to us, Catherine was in love with Henry and for her anything he did was deserving of praise.

Henry returned unharmed and triumphant to England and a very relieved Catherine in October 1513, but fell ill and was forced to take to his bed, recovering shortly after. Catherine's regency was over but she had proven herself every bit her mother's daughter.

The successes of 1513 allowed Henry and Catherine to turn to the safer art of diplomacy in 1514 and marriage often came hand in hand with that. Henry's sister, Princess Mary had been betrothed to Catherine's nephew, Charles, since 1507, but in a sudden about turn, the betrothal was broken off and she instead married the king of France Louis XII, a man old enough to be her father. The reason for this change was the souring of relations between England and Spain once again. Both of Charles' grandfathers, Ferdinand and Maximilian, wanted to postpone the marriage for the quite genuine reason of Charles' health, – he was only 14 at the time and had recently been ill. History had proven that it was perhaps best to err on the side of caution and not allow couples to marry too young, but Henry took it as a personal affront and broke off their engagement altogether.[17]

It did not help that Ferdinand was once again making a truce with France that threatened to leave England out in the cold. Whilst Henry has often been accused of whimsical behaviours, and it certainly looks like a whim to throw a great marital alliance away, by this time he was well versed in Ferdinand's tactics and decided enough was enough. Whilst the reason for Ferdinand's delay may have been genuine this time around, his previous behaviour did not inspire confidence in his son-in-law who, despite his recent invasion, also turned to France as an ally, leading to Mary's marriage to the French king. Catherine was horrified at the breakdown of relations with her home country. But she had also become wise to Ferdinand's manipulations, and whilst there was no open breach, she now considered herself Henry's wife and England's queen first. She was supported in this by some of her Spanish household. Fray Diego and Maria de Salinas were widely believed to have been the main sources of this stand, but it is unfair to suggest Catherine could not think for herself, especially after everything she had so far undertaken and achieved. Catherine was willing to listen to advice, but she could never be talked into doing anything that went against what she believed to be right. But it was far easier to blame the people around her for her decision, than the queen herself.

Mary departed for France in October 1514 and Catherine lost a sister-in-law and good friend, but it would turn out to be a short separation. Mary was queen of France for just under three months before her husband passed away, reportedly from over exertion in the marriage bed. She returned to England in May 1515, and despite her short reign, was known as the French Queen for the rest of her life.

Catherine experienced another loss in the same month when her confessor, Fray Diego, was expelled from England on the orders of her husband. Accusations had been made of gross misconduct, which included relationships with various ladies of the court and an ecclesiastical court convicted him of fornication, an act unthinkable in a confessor. Fray Diego did not go quietly, claiming he was ill-used and, interestingly, that Catherine was even more so. What is even more interesting is that, despite the ecclesiastical court's judgement, Catherine recommended him to her father but did not stop his expulsion from England. Catherine would not have dreamed of contradicting Henry, but if she believed her friar was at fault she would hardly have recommended him; neither would she have done so if she believed the court's judgement. It is most likely that something else was at play that has not come down to us. Perhaps with the passage of time she was able to remember past difficulties he had caused her and decided it was time to part ways, but not without a reward for his help and loyalty.[18]

Before Catherine could reunite with her friend and sister-in-law, she received the shocking news that Mary had remarried and without her brother's permission, or so it seemed. She had chosen as her husband Charles Brandon, Duke of Suffolk, Henry's closest friend, who had been sent to escort Mary back to England following her bereavement. The circumstances of their marriage are a little murky, but Mary had extracted a promise from Henry before leaving to marry the old king of France, that if she did her duty this time, next time she could choose a husband for herself, Henry agreed, though whether he expected his sister to hold him to it is another matter entirely, But she did, and the couple were married in France and an apprehensive Brandon wrote to Cardinal Thomas Wolsey stating that: 'And the Queen would never let me [be] in rest till I had granted her to be married; and so, to be plain with you, I have married her harettylle and has lyen wyet her, in soo moche [as] I fyer me lyes that sche by wyet chyld'.[19] Rumours were spreading that the new king of France, Francis I, was interested in the beautiful widow and he already had reputation for being a ladies' man that would grow throughout his reign. It may be for that reason, that Mary begged Charles to marry her in order to preserve her honour and allow her to return to England without fear of being dispatched by Henry to marry another stranger.

However, this is exactly what princesses had been doing for centuries and would continue to do so after the Tudors. It could be unpalatable, but was not unusual. Catherine had done her duty twice, unquestioningly, and believed it was her destiny to be married into England and become its queen and she had never wavered from that belief. Out of the two royal women, Catherine was the more conventional in this case.

But it is interesting to ponder why Mary thought she could do this? Aside from the promise she had from her brother, which he may not have honoured from choice or circumstances beyond his control, it just wasn't a decision a princess could make for herself. But perhaps the answer lies in another promise? Before being dispatched to escort his sister back to England, Henry had extracted a promise from Suffolk that he would not propose to her, so perhaps he was already aware of the man Mary had in mind when she extracted her promise from him, or he was aware of an affection between them before her marriage? If this is the case, was Catherine aware? It would seem strange for her not to be, given how close she and Mary were, but perhaps Catherine believed that Mary would do her duty as she had done. Either way, Charles' less than chivalrous and almost cowardly blame of Mary for the match, shows he was aware of the dangerous position he now found himself in. It was only following

Mary Tudor and Charles Brandon, Duke of Suffolk, attributed to Jan Gossaert, c.1515. This portrait was commissioned to celebrate their marriage, though their defiance of Henry and his royal prerogative could have landed them in serious trouble. (*Public Domain image, via Wikimedia Commons*)

an agreement that Mary surrender her dowry and the couple pay a large fine that the couple returned to Henry's court. They were officially married on 13 March 1515 at Greenwich Palace, with Henry and Catherine in attendance. Henry was usually angry when anyone crossed him, and he did lose a valuable diplomatic chess piece with his sister's second marriage, but he made quite a good profit out of their elopement and this possibly helped to placate him. All three surviving children of Henry VII and Elizabeth of York would buck the trend when it came to their marriages.

Catherine's attention to the family drama was temporarily diverted by the arrival of the Venetian ambassador, Sebastian Giustinian, whom she met and went riding with before he met her husband. This was an unusual break from protocol and a sign that Catherine's influence was a high as ever and worth cultivating; it was recognised that greeting her would please her husband. The May Day celebrations that year saw Catherine and her ladies riding into the woods where they were greeted by Henry and his men clad in green and carrying bows, in another allegory to Robin Hood. They dined there and enjoyed music before watching the king and his men joust.

October 1515 saw Henry and Catherine receiving the news that they could soon have another reunion on their hands. Henry's elder sister, Margaret, Queen of Scotland, had crossed the border back into England. Margaret had had difficulties following her husband's death at Flodden, and

Margaret Tudor, Queen of Scotland by Daniel Mijtens, c.1620–8. Margaret returned to England in 1515, where she received lavish gifts from her brother and sister-in-law. (*Public Domain image, via Wikimedia Commons*)

they had been compounded by her marriage to Archibald Angus, 6th Earl of Douglas. Margaret had become regent upon the accession of her son, James V, but her husband's will stated that she only retained the position so long as she remained unmarried. This was not an attempt by James IV to ensure Margaret remained loyal to his memory, but a canny understanding of the Scottish nobles at the time. Scotland was a difficult land to rule, and he knew that if Margaret married anyone within the kingdom, the old rivalries and jealousies he had fought to control would immediately break out and make her position untenable and this is exactly what happened. Following the arrival, from France, of the new regent, John Stewart, Duke of Albany, a cousin of James IV, Margaret had been required to surrender the king's person to him and that of her younger son, Alexander. This she sadly did in August 1515; following this parting, she made plans to escape to England.

Margaret was heavily pregnant when she arrived, and she gave birth to a daughter she named after herself shortly after. It took some time for her to recover from the birth and it appears her life was even feared for at one point. Worse was to come when she was informed of her younger son's death. Though when her English host, Lord Dacre, attempted to insinuate that Albany had had him killed in order to seize the throne, Margaret still had enough strength of mind to state that it didn't make sense for him to have done that; if he had done so it would have been her elder son, the king, who died. Margaret was clearly in Henry and Catherine's thoughts, as they sent her and her daughter lavish presents of clothes and jewellery for Christmas that year. It would not be until May 1516, at Greenwich Palace, that the Tudor siblings and Catherine would be reunited for the first time since 1503. Despite Catherine's role as regent when her husband was killed, Margaret does not appear to have held Catherine personally responsible. Catherine had sent a friar to Margaret shortly after James IV's death, to offer her condolences, and Margaret had graciously replied, thanking her for her sympathy and hoping to be remembered to her brother. Margaret would not return to Scotland until June 1517 and by that time she would have witnessed, or at least heard of, Catherine's intercession in the evil May Day Riots of 1517.

The May Day Riots were a culmination of several things, but mainly routed in xenophobia. The economy had recently experienced a downturn and the feared sweating sickness appeared to be spreading again and it was Foreign Merchants who bore the brunt of the frustration. English merchants were subjected to stricter rules than their foreign counterparts. This difference was compounded by their rivals' perceived arrogance and entitlement, and boiled over into a riot that involved around 2000 citizens vandalising and looting properties, before an army of soldiers was sent by Wolsey and the Lords to quell the insurrection. Around 300 rioters were arrested and their ring leaders were immediately executed, but on 14 May a group of around 400 were summoned to Westminster Hall. With halters around their necks, they were greeted by an imposing and angry looking Henry. Catherine was so moved by their plight that she knelt before her husband with tears in her eyes, begging him to pardon them, not for their sake but the women and children they would leave behind. Thomas Wolsey, by now a cardinal, also knelt and reiterated Catherine's plea, to which Henry, appearing moved by them both, allowed the prisoners to be released to the joy and celebration of witnesses. Following this display of intercession and mercy, the people's appreciation and love for Catherine were increased tenfold. But it was almost certainly planned beforehand and carefully stage managed by the king, the queen and cardinal to ensure maximum impact on the crowd and to reinforce Henry's authority.[20]

In July, a banquet and joust were held at Greenwich Palace to celebrate Charles and Maxmilian forming the League of the Defence of the Church. For the occasion Catherine wore 'cloth of gold with chains around [her] neck, everything glittered with gold'.[21] In a touching sign, Henry had organised for the jousters to wear outfits embroidered with their initials: H and K. The days following saw the English at their best – Henry's entire court showed off their finery, both clothing and jewellery, and danced and sang, treating their Spanish guests to every courtesy as if they were royalty themselves. It must have seemed like paradise, but it was not to last; days later the sweating sickness made a violent return.

It was suspected that Catherine's first husband, Arthur, had died of the sickness, and she may have suffered from it herself, so she knew first hand that the sickness had no respect for royalty, it killed indiscriminately. Henry and Catherine took immediate precautions to protect themselves, fleeing to the cleaner air in the countryside, taking only a much-reduced household and restricting visitors to essential figures only.[22] In 1551 a physician, John Caius, wrote a list of the symptoms and signs of the sweating sickness in his book *A Boke or Counseill Against the Disease Commonly Called the Sweate, or Sweatyng Sicknesse*. The symptoms included headaches, chills, dizziness, delirium, pain in the neck, shoulders and limbs, a rapid pulse, thirst, sweating and exhaustion. Unfortunately, there were no warning signs that you had caught it, you only knew once you started displaying the symptoms. If you lived past a day after first showing signs of it, there was a good chance you would survive. But catching it once did not provide immunity – a person could catch the sickness several times. The wave seemed to recede by January 1518, but it had taken some familiar figures from Henry and Catherine's court and it seemed that everyone knew someone who had lost someone.

The detail on a surviving suit of Henry's armour depicting Henry and Catherine's initials entwined. These often appeared on clothing, buildings, jewellery and much more. (*Author's collection*)

Catherine was reminded of Arthur again when the Pope wrote to her to intercede for her old confessor, Alessandro Geraldini. Geraldini had been recalled to Spain in 1502, following a letter he wrote stating that Arthur and Catherine's marriage had been consummated when Catherine insisted it had not. He was now attempting to return to England and Catherine, but she would not forgive him for his betrayal, even with the intercession of the Holy Father. As Catherine's confessor, Geraldini may have heard details from Catherine that led him to believe their marriage had been consummated. If that is where he got his information from, he had broken the seal of the confessional and that was unforgivable to Catherine. It is also completely possible he misunderstood what Catherine was attempting to tell him and she felt he was lying or untrustworthy.[23]

On 12 January 1519, the Emperor Maxmilian died, leaving the title of Holy Roman Emperor vacant. This title was not hereditary but elective and before his death he had tried to ensure that his grandson Charles would be elected. To be elected, the nominee required a majority vote from seven electors who were to elect a 'King of the Romans' who would then be crowned by the Pope, though the coronation was not always performed. Charles, Francis and even Henry all threw their hat into the ring, although it was realistically only a two-man contest between France and Spain. The election process involved a great deal of bribery, and England just didn't have the resources or the influence to ensure Henry's election, not that this ever seemed occur to him. In the end Charles would be elected, becoming the Emperor Charles V, his most recognised title, and making Catherine the aunt of the most powerful man in Christendom, a fact that would become relevant later.

Portrait of Emperor Charles V by Jakob Seisenegger, c.1532. (*Public Domain image, via Wikimedia Commons*)

Charles and Catherine would be fortunate to meet when Charles visited England in May 1520. The Emperor was travelling to his coronation in Rome when Henry arranged for a rendezvous in England, much to Catherine's excitement and happiness. Upon being told, she clasped her hands together and raised her eyes to the heavens and praised God 'for the grace she hoped he would do her that she might see Charles which was her greatest desire in the world',[24] and told his ambassador that 'her greatest desire was to see you [Charles] here and to receive you with the greatest honour and best cheer possible'.[25] She first clapped eyes on him in the Archbishops Palace at Canterbury, on 27 May. Charles, as was customary in Spain, asked for his aunt's blessing and Catherine gladly gave it, with tears in her eyes. Aunt, uncle and nephew enjoyed 4 days of celebrations before Charles departed for Flanders. Catherine and Henry had their own itinerary to keep as well, as they travelled to Dover Castle and there boarded a ship and travelled to Calais to meet with Henry and Charles' sometime rival, Francis I.

This meeting would come to be known as the Field of the Cloth of Gold as both kings tried to outdo each other in magnificence. A temporary palace was erected at Guîsnes to house the king and queen of England during their stay, the walls and roof of which were made of canvas, but the foundations and framework were of stone and timber with real glass for the windows. The palace included four separate sets of apartments to house Henry, Catherine, Mary and Cardinal Thomas Wolsey. Decor was not forgotten in the pursuit of function and practicality; the apartments were laid with rich silk carpets and expensive tapestries lined the walls. The ceiling too was hung with silk or was decorated with gilt and gold. The palace also had its own chapel, which was decorated with cloth of gold and golden ornaments, including candlesticks and basins. The chapel contained two closets, one each for Henry and Catherine to worship privately, and the closets themselves were decorated with precious stones and pearls. Catherine's altar held twelve great images of gold. The grounds were not forgotten – statues of ancient princes and heroes were placed around the palace and a gilded fountain poured red and white wine. A tiltyard for jousting and armed combat was built alongside hundreds of tents for the king and queen's household. In total, the palace had taken three months to build by 600 English and Flemish workers.

Francis I, king of France, by Jean Clouet, c.1527–30. (*Public Domain image, via Wikimedia Commons*)

Catherine and Henry each had an almost equally large retinue that had to be carefully balanced with that of King Francis and Queen Claude so as not provoke jealousies. Catherine's retinue included three bishops, four barons, three chamberers, fifty yeomen of the chamber, a duchess, seven countesses, sixteen baronesses, eighteen knights' wives and twenty-five gentlewomen. They each were entitled to bring a different number of their own servants, so it is easy to

A tapestry section depicting Francis I at the Field of the Cloth of Gold. One of the most magnificent and expensive events of Henrys reign, it achieved very little in the grand scheme of things. (*Public Domain image, via Wikimedia Commons*)

see how the number of people travelling with the king and queen soon mounted up. In total, the tents were able to accommodate around 820 people.

Catherine prepared an extensive wardrobe for the visit and her wardrobe account for the same year included payments for two pieces of eighty-six yards of long white satin, fifty-eight yards of green velvet, seventy-three yards of green Bruges satin, green, yellow and russet velvet, black, crimson velvet and green cloth of gold black sarcenet. She also ensured the people who served her were dressed well, buying fabrics in the Tudor colours of green and white to make coats and doublets for her guards and chamberers. She also paid for buckles, swords, shirts and points and for her ladies, coifs of gold.[26]

On 7 June, the two kings met on neutral ground in the Val d'Or (the Golden Valley), the French having travelled from their camp in Ardres. They greeted each other warmly, doffing their caps and dismounting their horses to embrace. They then entered a golden tent for a private meeting. On witnessing this friendly moment, tensions must have eased as they had been high on both sides – understandably given the history between England and France.

An odd story has come down to us that, to show his commitment, Henry had promised not to shave his beard until he and Francis met. However, Catherine apparently liked him clean shaven and convinced him not to pursue the idea. When Francis's mother, Louise of Savoy, heard of this, she confronted the English ambassador, a certain Sir Thomas Boleyn, who explained the situation. Apparently satisfied, Louise gamely replied that it did not matter too much because the kings' love for each other was 'not in their beards but in their hearts'.[27]

The English and French went on to enjoy eighteen days of combined banquets, jousting, theatrical entertainments, religious ceremonies and diplomacy. The two queens were required to play their part, mainly as hostesses, with Catherine hosting Francis in the English camp, with Mary's assistance, and Claude hosting Henry in the French, with the assistance of her mother-in-law. They gave prizes to the victors of each tournament or challenge but were also able to act in a diplomatic role, Catherine by virtue of her years of experience and Claude as the mother of two sons. The two queens' tact and diplomacy may have been needed when Henry rashly challenged Francis to a wrestling match which he promptly lost, much to his embarrassment.[28] He was able to recover some dignity when he beat Francis at archery.

On the penultimate day the kings and queens and their entire courts attended a religious Mass presided over by Wolsey, where the Chapel Royal Choirs from both England and France took turns to sing. To mark the end of the Mass, a large dragon made from canvas and wooden hoops created by the English flew above them from Ardres to Guîsnes. The dragon combined Francis' salamander emblem with Henry's Welsh Tudor dragon in a tribute to the new friendship between the two countries.[29] The visit concluded the next day, 24 June, with a final round of banquets before the French and English kings and queens bid farewell. The idea had been to create a lasting peace and friendship between the previously warring countries but a sign of how sincerely it was meant, by Henry at least, was revealed days later when he met Charles – once again – in Flanders. On 10 July, Henry and Catherine left Calais with a small entourage and crossed the border into Flanders where they were greeted by Charles and his aunt, Margaret, who acted as the Governor of the Netherlands on his behalf. This was a rare family reunion for Catherine as she had not seen Margaret for over twenty years. Charles and both his aunts and uncle travelled to Calais where they enjoyed banquets and masques held at the Exchequer and Staple Inn. The original idea of holding them in a specially built banqueting house had to be abandoned, as due to the bad weather it had not been completed. An agreement was reached that Henry and Charles would each have the same friends and enemies, and neither would enter a treaty without the knowledge of the other. On 14 July, Henry and Catherine set sail for England.[30]

The Field of the Cloth of Gold was a triumph in public relations and splendour, but its goal of peace and friendship was an expensive failure. Henry and Catherine met with her nephew and discussed alliances between them within days of its ending and it was well known that Charles and Spain had a difficult relationship with France – almost as difficult as England's – so when they agreed that their friend and enemies were the same, they were both talking about France. The cost was difficult to swallow as well; in 2020 it was calculated that the eighteen-day event cost the equivalent of around £15 million in today's money. But it's not just modern historians who thought it was a lot of money for little gain; observers at the time thought so too.

Margaret of Austria by Bernard Van Orley, c.1510–20. Catherine had not seen her sister-in-law since she had left Spain over twenty years previously. (*Public Domain image, via Wikimedia Commons*)

1521 was an important year for the Catholic Church. In January, Catherine's nephew convened the Diet of Worms. The Diet was an assembly that aimed to deal with the growing influence and works of the monk and teacher, Martin Luther, who openly criticised the Church. Several years earlier, on 31 October 1517, Martin Luther had published a work he called *Disputation on the Power of Indulgences* or *The Ninety-Five Theses* as it has become better known. Luther had become increasingly angry that the clergy were selling 'indulgences', which were promised remissions for sin and could be bought for someone living or already dead and who was believed to be in purgatory. His work attacked this practice and other papal abuses he had witnessed. Whilst there was a general agreement that some areas of the Church did need reform, some of Luther's ideas contradicted the Catholic Church's teachings and verged on heresy. For instance, he believed that people could be saved through their faith alone and not their own efforts. His statements challenged the Catholic Church's role as intermediary between the people and God. Luther was excommunicated by the Pope but appeared at the Diet in April under a promise of safe conduct, issued by Frederick III of Saxony. He refused to recant and was charged as a 'notorious heretic' and outlaw, making him a criminal.³¹

Henry, as a good son of the Church, was horrified by Luther's writings and set about writing his own work in the defence of the Church. The work would be titled the *Assertio Septem Sacramentorum* or *Defence of the Seven Sacraments* and it is largely considered his own, though he may have had assistance from Thomas More and Cardinal Wolsey. In his work he vehemently defended the Church and the Sacraments and, in some cases, used quite strong language to do so. A grateful Pope rewarded Henry with the title 'Fidei Defensor' or Defender of the Faith – a title that has been held by every English and British monarch since.³²

Catherine herself was staunchly Catholic and was equally horrified by Luther's writings. Could Henry have discussed his work with her? Catherine had been taught canon law, scripture, devotional literature and history and her reputation as an intelligent and educated woman was widely known. Erasmus himself said she was 'well instructed not merely in comparison of her sex and is no less to be respected for her piety than her erudition'. Catherine saw any attempts to eradicate heresy as God's work. As a child of Isabella and Ferdinand, it was unlikely she would ever think otherwise, and as she grew older she became more involved with the Church. Her reputation and influence were such that in 1523 she received a letter from Pope Adrian VI encouraging her to influence her husband:

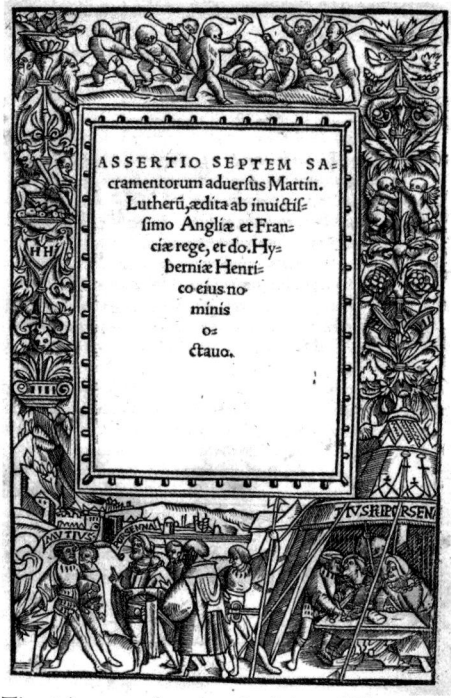

The title page of a printed edition of Henry VIII's *Assertio septem sacramentum or the Defence of the Seven Sacraments*, c. sixteenth century. Given Catherine's formidable education it's reasonable to suggest Henry may have discussed his ideas for the work with Catherine. (*Public Domain image, via Wikimedia Commons*)

> *All the world knows the zeal of the late King and Queen Catholic [Ferdinand and Isabella] in behalf of the Catholic faith, whose footsteps Katherine has followed. Is writing to the King her husband touching the oppression of Christendom by the loss of Rhodes. Begs she will give effect to his exhortations like a good Catholic, and induce him to peace, or at least some good truce, by means of which the power of the Turk may be repressed.*³³

The Church had been a great source of comfort during earlier troubles, and Catherine was known to keep many relics; in later years she would wear a habit of the order of St Francis under her clothes. For Luther to attack one of the mainstays of her world and something she held dear would have been like an arrow to her heart. But Catherine had proven she was equal to the task of defence, especially of something or someone she held dear. It is not a far-fetched idea that she may have offered suggestions or comments on Henry's work.

However, like her mother she was not blind to bad practice. Several

Catherine of Aragon by Lucas Horenbout, c.1525. (*Public Domain image, via Wikimedia Commons*)

smaller religious houses closed during Catherine's tenure as Queen, and whilst some appeared to be conveniently timed in order for Cardinal Wolsey to build his college on their former grounds, or their funds redistributed for the same cause, others did have genuine complaints made against them and when a house needed reforming or closing, she approved of the action taken.

Catherine saw her nephew for the third and last time in May 1522 when Charles visited England, this time staying for six weeks. Henry rode to greet him at Dover Castle on 28 May. The next day the two men enjoyed inspecting Henry's Navy, forcing Catherine to wait again to greet him which she did on 2 June at Greenwich Palace surrounded by the court. Amongst the usual feasting, dancing, hunting and jousting the two men signed a treaty that became known as the Treaty of Windsor, agreeing to invade France together in 1524 and providing for a marriage agreement for Henry and Catherine's daughter, Mary. Prior to the signing of the treaty a play was staged, in which Francis I was represented by a wild, proud horse and only the friendship and strength of Henry and Charles could tame him. Charles left England on 6 July, and though they would never meet again, Henry and Catherine would each be a presence and influence in his life in various ways for the rest of his life.[34]

Catherine had proven herself as an ambassador, intercessor, regent, wife and queen in almost every respect ... but she did not have a son.

Chapter 6

Motherhood

Catherine had six pregnancies throughout her life, but it is possible that there were ones that tragically were lost early on and not recorded. This would especially have been true later in her life when the need for an heir was becoming a matter of urgency.

The first sign that Catherine would have received that she may be pregnant would have been the ceasing of her 'courses' (periods). In Tudor times there was no sure way of knowing if a woman was pregnant and usually expectant mothers waited for their child's first movements in the womb, known as the quickening, before announcing the good news. This would have been especially true of royal women, when a whole dynasty and their country's future were depending on their fertility.[1]

A display depicting the dates of Catherine's known pregnancies and their tragic fates, at Hampton Court Palace. The date given here differs from what is now known for her fourth pregnancy. (*Author's collection*)

Sadly, Catherine's first pregnancy ended prematurely with a stillbirth on 31 January 1510. The baby was a daughter, but Catherine's stomach still stayed round and did not decrease in size, leading her physicians to believe that she had lost one of a pair of twins.[2] Four months later Fray Diego would write to Ferdinand to explain the unfortunate occasion and what happened next:

All the past time I did not dare to write to your Highness of the condition of the Queen my Lady, in order not to annoy her, and because all the physicians deceived themselves until time was the judge of the truth. The last day of January in the morning her Highness brought forth prematurely a daughter, without any other pain except that one knee pained her the night before. This affair was so secret that no one knew it until now, except the King my Lord, two Spanish women, a physician and I. The physician said that her Highness remained pregnant of another child, and it was believed and kept secret.[3]

In preparation for giving birth, Catherine ceremonially took to her chamber in March. 'Taking to her Chamber' was the occasion when a queen retired from public life and retreated to her chambers to await the birth of her child, with only her female servants for company. Not even the King was allowed to enter. This process was also known as 'lying-in' or 'confinement' and usually took place a month before the baby was due to arrive. However, no baby arrived and Catherine's courses had already resumed and the swelling, likely the result of some sort of postpartum infection, disappeared shortly after, leaving a very embarrassed Henry and Catherine to try and explain away what had happened.

This is another good example of how little pregnancy and its symptoms and complications were understood at this time, and no blame can be attached to Catherine and Henry who were likely both each other's first sexual partner; such things as 'the talk' would have been unthinkable. That's not to say they were left with no knowledge of the facts of life but what they were taught would have been very limited.

Fray Diego finished his letter with a glimpse of Henry and Catherine's relationship, reinforcing their love and commitment towards one another:

Her Highness is very healthy, and the most beautiful creature in the world, with the greatest gaiety and contentment that ever was. The King my Lord adores her, and her Highness him. Your Highness is bound to give many thanks to our Lord that he gave you two such Christian children in their Graces my Sovereigns, so very wise, learned, and with all the natural perfections above all others.[4]

However, the couple did go on to have their first marital spat soon after. One of the sisters of the Duke of Buckingham, Anne, had caught the king's eye and was 'much liked by the king, who went after her'. To try and be discreet, Henry had his close friend William Compton intercede for him and the pair were colluding so well it left observers unsure who was really pursuing Anne. Her elder sister, Elizabeth, became concerned at the situation and brought it to her brother's attention. He then furiously confronted Compton, who reported what had happened to Henry. Henry, furious that a bit of light-hearted fun had become a public scandal, reprimanded the duke, who angrily left the court. Anne's husband followed him, taking her with him and reportedly placed her in a convent 'that no one may see her'. Henry turned his anger on Elizabeth, and she and her husband were banished from court. Elizabeth and Anne's absence was noted by Catherine, who asked Henry what had happened which led to a disagreement. Afterwards the whole court knew that 'the queen was vexed with the king, and the king with her, and thus this storm went on between them'.[5]

Catherine had perhaps hoped that Henry would be different than other men, especially given the love and affection they shared, but Henry was very much a product of his time and Catherine soon learned she would have to adapt herself and turn a blind eye to maintain a good relationship with her husband. She would not make a complaint of one of his affairs again, not until a lot more was at stake.

Instead, she turned her mind to her new pregnancy. Catherine had fallen pregnant again quite quickly and this time she would take to her chamber at Richmond Palace just before Christmas where, on 1 January 1511, she gave birth to a healthy son named Henry after his proud father. The new prince immediately became Duke of Cornwall at his birth. The Tower of London fired the traditional royal salute and Henry insisted Catherine's midwife receive a cash reward. He also instructed the Lord Mayor to organise wine for the citizens of London to toast to the health of his son.

On 6 January, Prince Henry was baptised at the Church of the Observant Friars that stood next to Richmond Palace. As protocol dictated, his parents were not in attendance – in fact Henry was 100 miles away in Norfolk, giving thanks for his son at the shrine of Our Lady at Walsingham – but almost the rest of the court would have been. The baby's godparents were William Warham, Archbishop of Canterbury, Louis XII of France and Catherine's sister-in-law, Margaret of Austria; though the latter two couldn't attend, they sent expensive gifts.

After the ceremony, the more distinguished guests, including the representative of the Doge of Venice and the ambassadors of Spain, France and the Vatican, greeted Catherine in her chambers and congratulated her on her son's birth. Catherine would not leave confinement until she had undergone a ceremony called the Churching. The Churching ceremony was a thanksgiving service that acknowledged the pains and trouble a new mother had been through and thanked God for her continuing health. It also represented a mother's re-entry to society after childbirth; she was now cleansed and purified. Catherine underwent her ceremony on 2 February and afterwards was able to take part and enjoy the celebrations for her son's birth. These would even surpass Prince Edward's celebrations over 25 years later.

Henry and Catherine travelled to Westminster where Henry had planned a tournament in his son's honour. The event lasted two days and Henry, calling himself 'Loyal Heart', rode in the lists in honour of his wife, winning prizes on the second day, Catherine was in her element, looking on at her adoring husband, acceding to the requests of the challengers and defenders and distributing prizes as

Detail of Henry VIII jousting in front of Catherine of Aragon to celebrate the birth of their son and heir, Prince Henry. From the *1511 Westminster Tournament Roll*. (*Public Domain image, via Wikimedia Commons*)

lady bountiful. She was also greeted with a pageant pulled onto the tiltyard by mythical beasts led by wild men that depicted a golden castle surrounded by a beautiful forest. Whilst everyone was admiring the contraption, its sides burst open and four armed knights with their tappers depicting golden pomegranates appeared; one of the knights was later to revealed to be Loyal Heart himself – to no one's surprise but Catherine's evident delight.

On the second day the jousts continued. This time Henry and his men rode under canopies of gold and purple velvet embroidered with the letters H and K in gold, Henry's canopy was distinguished by the Imperial Crown topping it, whilst the others were topped with the letter K. That night a banquet was held, followed by singing and dancing and another pageant featuring lords and ladies dressed in white and purple satin with cloth of gold; their

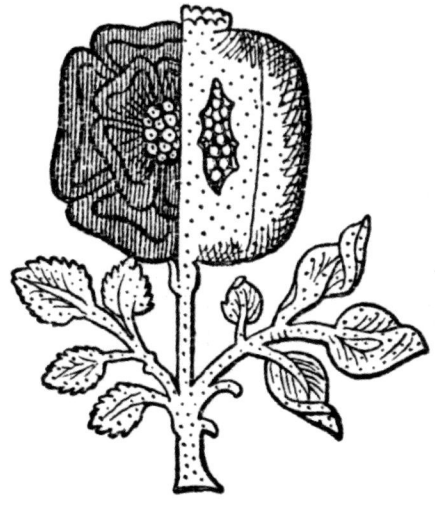

Compound Badge of Henry VIII and Catherine of Aragon, from the Westminster Tournament Roll. These could be worn by people who worked for the king and queen to identify them as their servants or even courtiers to show their loyalty. (*Public Domain image, via Wikimedia Commons*)

garments again glittering with the by now familiar H and K of the king and queen. The excitement clearly overcame Henry who spontaneously invited the observers to help themselves to the gold decorations on the costumes, including his own, an offer that was eagerly taken up and in the end, required the royal guards to step in and break up after a few bystanders got hurt though not seriously. By this time Catherine and Henry had retreated to safety and it was all treated as light-hearted fun.

This was the happiest time of Catherine's life; she had achieved everything she had set out to do. She was the queen she believed God had wanted her to be, her husband and his people, now hers as well, had welcomed and adored her. She was the mother of the heir to the throne and could look forward to giving him brothers and sisters. England and Spain were allies, united in common goals and interests, but also by familial ties that would only be strengthened in the future.

Then it all came crashing down.

Just ten days after the celebrations at Westminster, Catherine and Henry received the terrible news that their son had died at Richmond; he was only 52 days old. We don't know what killed the prince, whether he caught an infection or if it was tragically what we know today as Sudden Infant Death Syndrome (SIDS) which has no known definitive cause. Whatever took his life left his parents equally devastated, though Henry 'dissimuled the matter ... the more to comfort the queen' who was heartbroken. Catherine 'like a naturall woman, made much lamentacioun' and it was believed to be largely thanks to Henry's support that she was able to get through this difficult time: 'by the kings good persuasion and behaviour her sorrow was mitygated' but it was 'not shortlye'.

As was custom, his mother and father did not attend his funeral but they ensured their young son received a grand ceremony to mark his status. Westminster Abbey had been chosen as his final resting place and the prince was carried from Richmond by water; his barge and two others were decorated almost entirely with black cloth. Payments were made for banner-painters, palls, a hearse, a canopy and over 5000 lbs of wax were provided for the candles and the torches, and 180 poor people were paid to pray for his soul. Henry Stafford, Earl of Wiltshire, Henry Bourchier, Earl of Essex and Thomas Grey, Marquis of Dorset acted as the Chief Mourners, and Sir Thomas Boleyn was in attendance acting as a pallbearer. The young prince was laid to rest in Westminster Abbey on the north side of the sanctuary, near the entrance to the Chapel of St Edward the Confessor.[6] Any memorial or marker Henry had constructed for his son had

Christchurch Gate at Canterbury Cathedral. Sixth from the left are the arms of the short-lived Prince Henry, Duke of Cornwall, son of Henry and Catherine of Aragon, central the arms of King Henry VIII and tenth from the left are the arms of Catherine of Aragon. (*Attribution Peter K. Burian, Wikimedia, CC 3.0; Public Domain image, via Wikimedia Commons*)

been lost by the 1860s when quite by accident, during the construction of the new high altar, his tiny coffin was rediscovered, but thankfully left undisturbed.[7]

Henry and Catherine had come together in their loss and had drawn strength from each other. Sadly at this time it was not unusual to lose a child or children – around seventeen per cent of children in Tudor England would die before reaching the age of one.[8]

It would not be until early 1513 that Catherine would fall pregnant again. This third pregnancy also ended in tragedy though it is unclear on what date. A document in the Venetian Calendar of State Papers records that 'a male heir was born to the king of England and will inherit the crown, the other son having died'. It appears that, like his brother, this baby boy was born alive but tragically died shortly after – even sooner than his brother given the lack of recorded celebrations. The account gives us the date of birth as 17 September but Catherine was on the move at this time, travelling between Woburn and Walsingham following the Battle of Flodden and did not enter a period of confinement or lying-in following the birth so it is likely she gave birth later once she was 'home'. Interestingly, Henry was also still in France so this points to the baby being premature as he would not have wanted to miss the birth of his heir after the loss of his last one. It's possible that the date is incorrect and these events occurred slightly later; communication across the country, let alone the Continent could be slow and easily distorted, so while the events may be correct the date perhaps is not.[9]

Catherine suffered another loss in November 1514 when she went into premature labour at around eight months. This time the child, another boy, was stillborn. Again, the Venetian State Papers provide us with an account written by the ambassador, Sebastian Giustinian, who wrote 'The Queen has been delivered of a stillborn male child of eight months to the very great grief of the whole court'.[10] Edward Hall's Chronicle contains a brief mention: 'in November, the queen was delivered of a prince which lived not long after'. Confirmation the birth was again premature was given by Pedro Martir in Spain who wrote bluntly 'the Queen of England had given birth to a premature child'.

By Catherine's fifth pregnancy everyone was on knife edge, including her husband, so much so that when the sad news arrived of her father's death, it was kept from her until the baby was born.[11] Ferdinand died on January 23, 1516, aged 63, in Madrigalejo (Cáceres). He was survived by his young widow, Germaine of Foix, three of his children with Isabella and a handful of illegitimate children born both before and during his marriage to Catherine's mother. Ferdinand had remarried to neutralise the French threat and in the hope of producing a male heir to protect his legacy of Aragon, Naples and Sicily. The couple did produce a son, but he died shortly after birth and Ferdinand's eldest surviving daughter,

Juana, inherited his lands. As with Castile, Juana never ruled, her place taken this time by her eldest son Charles, following the continued rumours of her instability and madness.

On 18 February, Catherine gave birth to a healthy child, a daughter, at Greenwich Palace. Henry and Catherine were ecstatic and despite the losses that had come before, Henry remained optimistic and was recorded as saying: 'if it was a daughter this time, by the grace of God, the sons would follow'.[12] They named their daughter Mary, and on 21 February she was christened in the Church of Friars Observant next to the palace. The Duchess of Norfolk, the Countess of Devon and Cardinal Wolsey were her godparents[13] and Catherine's old friend, Margaret Pole, now the Countess of Salisbury in her own right, acted as her sponsor.[14] Following her christening, Lady Margaret Bryan was appointed to oversee Mary's care and, in 1520, the Countess would be appointed Mary's governess.

Sadly, Henry's hope for the future would be crushed, Catherine did become pregnant again, but sadly went into labour prematurely and suffered another stillbirth on 9 November 1518; the baby would have been a princess. Giustinian wrote: 'This night the Queen was delivered of a daughter, to the vexation of

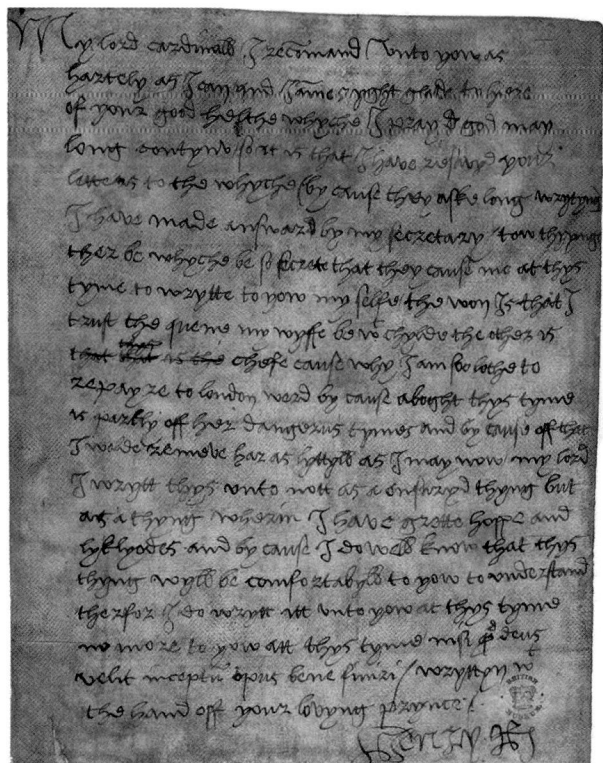

A letter written to Cardinal Thomas Wolsey by Henry VIII, c. June 1518. In it he expresses his anxiety for Catherine's pregnancy. Sadly for them both it would be unsuccessful and her last. (*British Library; Public Domain image, via Wikimedia Commons*)

as many as knows it as the entire nation looked for a prince'.[15]

Catherine didn't know it yet, but she would never conceive again. To make matters worse, Henry's mistress, Lady Elizabeth (Bessie) Blount, had given birth to a healthy son, to Henry's great happiness. He immediately recognised the child as his, calling him Henry Fitzroy – Fitzroy meaning 'Son of King'. It's not clear when Henry and Bessie began a flirtation, as Henry was unusual amongst his royal contemporaries in that he was quite discreet in his affairs, but the child must have been conceived around the time Catherine herself was nearing the end of her last pregnancy, as Fitzroy was born in June 1519. His birth was not reported by ambassadors at the time, indicating that it was kept a secret, despite Henry's recognition of him. But by 1525 the whole world knew of his existence when he was made a Knight of the Garter and created Duke of Richmond and Somerset.[16]

Close up of Maria of Aragon from a stained-glass window in the High Chapel of the Church of Saint Mary of Victory (Batalha Monastery, Leiria, Portugal), attributed to Francisco Henriques, *c*.1510–13. Maria's death left only Juana and Catherine as the surviving children of Isabella and Ferdinand. (*Public Domain image, via Wikimedia Commons*)

When Catherine learnt of the little boy's existence is also a mystery, but after the arguments and recriminations that had followed their spat over his mistress in 1510, Catherine clearly did not confront Henry for his unfaithfulness. Perhaps she reasoned that it was normal for kings to have illegitimate children. She had been aware of her father's, and after all a mistress could not threaten a wife's position, no matter if she had a son.

Just over a year after Mary's birth, Catherine would lose another link with her homeland, when her sister Maria died, aged 34, on 7 March 1517 in Lisbon, Portugal. Maria was perhaps the most successful and luckiest of Isabella and Ferdinand's children. She married her elder sister's widow, Manuel I of Portugal, and produced ten children with him during seventeen years of marriage, eight of which survived to adulthood. Amongst them she could boast two kings, an empress and two cardinals. She was not a political figure but was known and respected for her pious conduct and good relations with her husband's family.[17]

Chapter 7

Anne Boleyn and The King's Great Matter

In 1525 Catherine's courses stopped, and it was realised she would never have another child. The heir to the throne of England was the Princess Mary and she would need to be educated as such. Catherine, who had seen how skilfully a female ruler could wield power, saw absolutely no problem with this and set about with her accustomed thoroughness to ensure her daughter was educated as the future queen regnant she was.

Catherine commissioned the Spanish Humanist, Juan Luis Vives, to write a manual on educating a princess and his work, *De Institutione Feminae Christianae* or *The Education of a Christian Woman* helped form the basis of her daughter's

Juan Luis Vives by an unknown artist, c. fifteenth century. (*Public Domain image, via Wikimedia Commons*)

education. Whilst Vives believed women should be properly educated, he also believed they were to be subjugated to their male relatives, whether it be a father or husband; in this he was no different than others of his time. His work recommended that women should always be virtuous, charitable and focused on domesticity and whilst the first two traits could be applied to a future queen consort, the latter trait would prove harder to accommodate in a ruler of England.

He provided a list of reading material as well – Mary should be encouraged to read the Bible and classical works including Cicero, Plato and Seneca rather than chivalric romances, which could warp her way of thinking. She was also to learn the domestic arts of embroidery, spinning and cooking.[1]

Catherine herself likely recognised that Mary would need more than this to be successful in her future, so Vives followed up his treaty with another in 1524 titled *De Ratione Studii Puerilis* or *On a Plan of Study for Children* which focussed more on languages and works on governing the commonwealth. Mary would grow up to speak Spanish, French, Latin, Greek and could understand Italian. Interestingly, there is a possibility she was taught Latin by the distinguished scholar and physician, Thomas Linacre. Linacre had been appointed as physician to Henry VIII upon his accession, but prior to this he had travelled around Italy and held a recognised reputation across Europe for his interest in the Greek language and medicine. At the time Mary was expanding her studies, he had already published two works on Latin grammar and was about to complete a third one for more advanced students. Marys own extensive abilities in Latin may have begun with him.[2]

Portrait of Desiderius Erasmus of Rotterdam by Quinten Metsys, c.1517. (*Public Domain image, via Wikimedia Commons*)

But Catherine evidently taught her daughter some of her Latin herself, as she later wrote to her:

> *As for your writing in Latin I am glad you shall change from me to master Federston, for that shall do you much good, to learn by him to write right. But yet sometimes I would be glad when you do write to Master Federston of your own inditing when he hath read it that I may see it. For it shall be a great comfort to me to see you keep your Latin and fair writing and all.*[3]

Her reading material now expanded too, becoming more ambitious, and included works by Thomas More and the Christian Humanist, Erasmus. Erasmus was a great admirer of Catherine and he dedicated his work *Christiani Matrimonii Institutio* or *The Institution of Christian Marriage* to her, writing:

> … *your qualities are known to us … we expect a work no less of your daughter Mary. For what should we not expect from a girl who is born of the most devout of parents and brought up under the care of such a mother?*

Vives also evidently believed Catherine was well suited to educate her daughter as he wrote:

… time will admonish her as to more exact details, and thy singular wisdom will discover for what they should be.

It was not all work and no play for Mary, she inherited her father's love of music and had an excellent singing voice complimented by a natural talent for dancing. She received praise for her skill playing the lute and virginals and enjoyed outdoor activities, such as riding, hunting and hawking, which was as much for exercise and her health as her enjoyment. Mary would turn out to be an able and precocious student, a fact that is often overshadowed by her more famous half-sister Elizabeth's education, and Catherine could look on with satisfaction as she grew into a young lady and a princess England could be (and was) proud of.

However, kings wanted male heirs and in this Henry was no different from his counterparts. Women were not barred from inheriting the English throne, but it was an outcome most strove to avoid where possible.

Henry had an illegitimate son, but it flew against all he knew and had been taught to promote an illegitimate son to such a position. The laws of England were clear that illegitimate children had no right to property as they were essentially 'children of no one'; it would have been especially difficult for Fitzroy to inherit the crown of England. It was also unclear if the people of England would accept such a blatant act either. Henry himself would later prove how essential it was for his heirs to be recognised as legitimate. Later things would reach a level of desperation and Fitzroy's candidature would be given more thought, but that time was not yet.

Instead Henry promoted both of his children. In 1525, he made his son Duke of Richmond and Somerset, an act that caused Catherine concern as Richmond had been the title that Henry's father had held before his accession. Shortly after, her fears appeared to be mollified as he sent their 9-year-old daughter to preside over the Council of Wales. Mary was never officially invested as the Princess of Wales but this move tacitly acknowledged that she was the heir to the throne and being prepared for her future.[4]

Princess Mary Tudor by Hans Holbein the Younger, year unknown. Mary was Catherine's only surviving and much-loved child. (*Public Domain image, via Wikimedia Commons*)

Whilst Catherine and Mary did not live together in the modern sense, the Welsh border was a lot further away than the palaces mother and daughter normally stayed in, and it will have been a wrench for Catherine to send her only child away. But it will have been mixed with pride knowing her daughter was following the traditional path of the heir to the throne of England.

Did she take a minute to remember her own brief sojourn there? If she did, was she able to reassure her daughter on their impending separation? Whilst Mary doesn't appear to have lived at Ludlow itself, though her council was based there, it probably would have been enough of an association to make Catherine recall her earlier years. Catherine's experience of the Marches had been tinged with triumph and sadness so she would have had mixed feelings and memories of the place where she had lost her first husband and almost her destiny, but she likely did not pass these onto Mary, Arthur was the past and Henry and Mary were her present and her future, and Catherine was a forward thinking woman. It would be later that the past would start haunting her.

For now, there was good news to celebrate; Charles had just defeated Francis I at the Battle of Pavia and taken the French king hostage. With France in disarray, it seemed that the moment was now right for Henry to try again to claim his French inheritance and he made overtures to Charles to that effect. He envisioned a joint invasion where he would take the crown and then he and Charles would divide the territory between themselves. Charles, however, was not interested in prolonging the war, nor was he keen to devote his own resources to this goal when he believed he could make better terms with his captured enemy. To Henry's disappointment, Francis would be released in 1526 after signing a humiliating treaty and delivering his two sons into Charles' care to act as hostages and ensure his compliance.[5] At around the same time, Charles broke his engagement to Mary and married another cousin, Isabella of Portugal, a daughter of Maria of Aragon, Catherine and Juana's sister.[6]

How often did Catherine and Henry discuss their daughter's future? They were not just her mother and father, they were also the king and queen of a realm; their lives were not just their own, their country literally depended on them and their child. It would not have just been Henry and Catherine discussing the future, but the king's council and his nobles, too. Any concerns each of the groups had about a future queen regnant would have been answered easily in Catherine's mind using just one example: her mother.

Isabella of Castile had fought for and won her throne, and, more importantly, she had kept it. She had been recognised as one half of the most powerful couple of the fifteenth and sixteenth centuries. She had not led her armies into the field, but Isabella had provided indispensable support to her husband who had, by ensuring they had more than adequate weapons, supplies, food and medical care. She had often been invited by Ferdinand to the army camps to see and greet her soldiers, Ferdinand knew Isabella was the best morale booster he had, and she was capable of inspiring loyalty and devotion amongst her people. She was an equal partner in her marriage and often counselled and revised treaties and wrote to fellow monarchs in her own right; there was no reason Mary could not have the same future. Isabella herself was the first queen regnant in Castile since her predecessor, Berengaria of Castile, in the thirteenth century so Castile did not have much experience of female rule either and had to learn to adapt, which it had done.

Catherine would not even countenance the argument that there was fear of a return to the recent turbulence in English history if a woman ruled England. Isabella had inherited the throne from a weak and vacillating king and had proven she was a better ruler than her brother, whose reign had seen power and respect eroded from the crown.

What Henry could have done was arrange for Mary to be married at a suitable age, thereby ensuring, God willing, she had children, one of which may have been a grandson who could inherit his throne. However, whomever Mary married would naturally expect to have a role and say in the governance of England on behalf of his wife and child. It would also mean the end of the Tudor dynasty and the arrival of a new, unknown royal house – not an outcome Henry wished to contemplate, let alone allow.

No one saw Henry's next course of action coming, though it began as a course of action in the loosest possible sense. In the late 1520s Henry fell in love again, and it wasn't with his wife.

In 1522, a young woman returned to the English court from France; her name was Anne Boleyn and she was the younger daughter of the experienced courtier and ambassador, Sir Thomas Boleyn and Lady Elizabeth Howard, the sister of the current Duke of Norfolk. Anne had been sent abroad by her father to be educated at the court of Catherine's sister-in-law, Margaret of Austria, the Governor of the Netherlands. Thomas had evidently made a good impression during his own sojourn

Anne Boleyn from a near contemporary portrait currently at Hever Castle, the Boleyn family home. Attributed to the British School, *c.*1550. Anne refused to become Henry's mistress so he offered her marriage, setting in motion a chain of events that would change Catherine's life forever. (*Public Domain image, via Wikimedia Commons*)

there in 1512, which led to Margaret's offer of a place in her household for one of his daughters.

Margaret's court was one of the most cultured and refined during the Renaissance and she often took in young girls and provided them with an extensive education. In her household, Anne learnt arithmetic and history alongside grammar, reading and writing. Domestic skills were not forgotten as Margaret ensured her charges were taught about household management, needlework, music, singing and manners. They also learnt to ride and hunt, falconry and archery, and for gentler pastimes the ladies were taught to play chess and cards. Anne remained at Margaret's court until 1513, when her father arranged for her to travel to France to serve its future queen, the younger sister of Henry VIII.

Anne remained in France for seven years following the death of King Louis of France, swiftly transferring to the new Queen Claude's household. During that time she became fluent in French, absorbing its culture, art and fashion; later it was commented that she could be taken for a French-born woman. She developed a lifelong interest in French literature, music and religious philosophy and became skilled in the art of courtly love.

Anne returned to England in 1522, when she was recalled by her father who was negotiating a marriage for her with a cousin, an Irishman named James

Catherine of Aragon witnessing Henry VIII and Anne Boleyn's growing love from Eleanor Fortesque Brickdale's *Golden book of Famous Women* c.1919. (*Public Domain image, via Wikimedia Commons*)

Butler. The marriage was intended to settle the dispute over the Earldom of Ormond following the death of the seventh earl. As the son of the former earl's eldest daughter, Anne's father believed he had the right to inherit. But a great-great grandson of the third earl disagreed, and claimed the earldom for himself. The marriage never came about and it's unclear why, as Henry himself wasn't interested in Anne at that point and was likely involved in an affair with her older sister, Mary, at this time.

Anne made her debut at the English court in a pageant titled the Chateau Vert, which was held in honour of the Imperial ambassadors. The pageant's characters included the different virtues, with the king's sister playing the part of Beauty, Mary Boleyn was Kindness, Anne was Perseverance and their future sister-in-law, Jane Parker, was Constancy. The pageant was a success and Anne quickly became one of the stars of Henry's court, attracting many admirers including the famous Tudor poet, Sir Thomas Wyatt, and Henry Percy, Earl of Northumberland.[7]

We don't know when exactly Anne first caught Henry's eye but to Catherine it was no cause for concern. Whilst hurtful, Henry had had mistresses before and had grown tired of them; this would just be another example of this and Catherine, with her usual wifely obedience, was obliged to submit. She had seen her mother tolerate her own father's affairs and they had not destroyed their loving relationship.

Henry did not intend at this stage to make Anne his wife and queen; he wanted her to become his mistress but Anne refused, shocking him. Whilst being the king's mistress could be considered an honour, it was a role full of knife edges and pitfalls and Anne, like Catherine, had also witnessed Henry tiring of his mistresses and wanted more for herself. She did not want her children to be illegitimate, nor did she want an uncertain future for herself and them. Besides, Henry was not overly generous with his mistresses either. Luckily for Anne, she managed to refuse him without hurting his feelings and on some occasions even left the court, but her refusal only increased his appetite for her, resulting in an impressive series of passionate letters that Henry sent to Anne. Some of these still survive in the Vatican Archives today, likely smuggled out of England by a supporter of Catherine. He constantly sent her gifts and even the results of his hunting expeditions, hoping she would think of the hunter when she did consume the food.

A desperate Henry even went so far as to offer to create an official post of 'King's Mistress' for her but Anne refused again. She had maintained her honour all these years and would not surrender it even for a king; she would only surrender it to her husband once she had one. With this final refusal, Henry took the unprecedented step of offering her marriage. Anne must have been shocked,

Kings did not marry their subjects, although there was a recent precedent with the marriage of Henry's own grandparents, King Edward IV and Elizabeth Woodville, but that had caused its own problems. Henry's circumstances were different to Edward's too – he was a married man and his wife was descended from an impressive royal dynasty of her own and had ties to some of the most powerful families in Europe. She was also much loved by the people of England.

But Anne had very little choice in the matter, the king had not lost interest in her and whilst she remained the object of his desire, she was not going to be approached by any other man or his family. On the other hand, to be a queen must have been a dazzling prospect for an educated woman such as Anne. A woman's duty was to marry for the benefit of her family and she could not marry higher than a king – so Anne accepted.[8]

But first Catherine had to be set aside.

Henry instructed Wolsey to secretly set up an ecclesiastical trial to investigate his marriage to Catherine, claiming his conscience was troubling him as she had been his brother's widow when he married her and therefore their marriage was unlawful and incestuous. His proof was that they had been unable to produce any healthy sons. Henry was also able to provide a biblical verse that supported him in this belief in Leviticus (20:21), which read:

If a man shall take his brother's wife, it is an unclean thing: he has uncovered his brother nakedness. They shall be childless.

Henry and Catherine were not, of course, childless as they did have a daughter but either Henry or his councillors decided to interpret childless to mean a lack of male issue. Interestingly, the Bible contradicts itself later in another book, Deuteronomy, verse 20:6, which reads:

… the wife of the deceased shall not marry to another, but his brother shall take her and raise up seed for his brother.

Reassuringly for Henry, in case Catherine or someone on her behalf took it into their head to use this reasoning against him, Henry's councillors advised him that Leviticus took precedence over Deuteronomy in canon law. However, there was also the question of the actual consummation itself – was Catherine and Arthur's marriage ever actually consummated? Catherine insisted it wasn't, so were they man and wife on paper only? They were publicly put to bed together but only two people knew what exactly happened in the chamber that night and every night following, and one of them was dead.

Henry always maintained that his scruples over marrying his brother's widow was the only reason he pursued an annulment of his marriage to Catherine, but he was seemingly blind to the fact that the people around him were well aware of his feelings for Anne and were smart enough to realise that his scruples had conveniently appeared when she agreed to marry him. He would later add that he needed a son to succeed him and Catherine could not give him one, but it is important for us to remember that Henry wanted Anne to be his mistress first, not his wife and queen. He only offered her marriage when she refused him. Henry was extremely gifted at convincing himself his causes were noble and right even when they weren't. More proof lies in his choice of future wife – if Henry's marriage to Catherine was invalid because of her prior relationship with Arthur, then a marriage to Anne would also be invalid by virtue of his prior affair with her sister.

Henry and Anne seemed to have operated under the assumption that once they had taken the necessary steps to secure an annulment of his marriage and presented Catherine with a *fait accompli*, she would retreat with perhaps a suitable allowance or agreement in place …they were both wrong.

Catherine quickly became aware of the plot against her and was horrified. She had been a loyal and dutiful wife for over twenty years, she had made England and its people her own, defending and protecting them as regent and queen consort, and had often put England before her homeland. She had tolerated Henry's mistresses and not loved him any less, taking genuine pleasure in the time they spent together talking, dining, celebrating, praying and raising their daughter. They had faced and mourned their losses together and comforted each other. Catherine had done anything and everything he asked without complaint and always put him first. Now after all that he was attempting to set her aside.

Catherine immediately wrote to her nephew informing him of the proceedings against her but did not confront her husband; instead when she saw him, she greeted him as she always did with a smile. Catherine knew that whilst Henry believed she was unaware of his activities, it bought her some time to prepare her own response and to take advice from her allies and supporters.

Reality hit Catherine when Henry finally approached her with his doubts on 22 June 1527, and whilst she had been aware, to hear them voiced out loud to her face must have been like a kick to the stomach. Henry informed her bluntly that they had been living in mortal sin throughout their entire marriage and that she must retire to a convent.[9] Quite why he approached Catherine, or anyone, like this is a mystery; perhaps his nerves got the better of him or perhaps he thought that the quicker he came out with it, the quicker everything would be better for them all. In any case it's not what happened.

We have two accounts of Catherine's response. One states that she burst into tears, unnerving her husband who lamely attempted to comfort her by saying that all would be done for the best and asking her to keep the whole business a secret, before he essentially ran away and left her to her heartbreak. Another account comes from the Spanish Chronicle, a document of dubious reliability in some areas that did include moments of truth, which has Catherine responding:

> *My good Henry, I well know whence all this comes and you know that the King Don Ferdinand, when he gave me in marriage with the Prince of Wales, was still young, and I came to the country a very young girl, and the good Prince only lived half a year after my coming. My father, the king Don Ferdinand, sent at once for me, but King Henry VII wrote and asked my father that I might marry you. You know how we were both agreed, and how my father sent to Rome for the dispensation, which the Pope gave, and which my father left well-guarded in Spain.*

It is worth remembering at this point that a precedent for a sibling marrying another sibling's widow existed within Catherine's own family: Maria had married Manuel I after their eldest sister's death, and that first marriage had been consummated as they had had a son together. A dispensation had been provided to allow the second marriage, and they had gone on to have a successful marriage and produced numerous children.

It's unclear when Catherine became aware that Henry had a replacement for her already waiting on the sidelines. Worse than that, she was not even a woman of royal blood but a member of the court who had served them, which meant that once Catherine did became aware she was doubly horrified. Catherine was the descendant of two monarchs of ancient royal lines, a queen anointed in the sight of God, and here was a young upstart threatening to undo the accepted order that had been in place for hundreds of years. In the years to come Catherine would always blame Anne for Henry's actions towards her and believed he had simply been led astray by her. To be fair to her this was not entirely self-delusion, many others also blamed Anne for Henrys actions. It would only be later that the people around Henry would be forced to confront the truth – that it was Henry who led and others were forced to follow. The clergy and lords that were assembled to try the marriage in England were unable to reach a conclusion, and thus the Pope was going to have to become involved.

Henry's desire for secrecy was soon brushed aside when Charles made it clear that he would be supporting his aunt wholeheartedly, and by strange coincidence he had the advantage. Charles' troops had been fighting a war against Francis I but they had not been fed or paid for several weeks. Understandably tempers soon ran high and on 6 May they boiled over when over 30,000 troops breeched the walls of Rome and ransacked the city. Pope Clement VII was forced to flee to the Castel Santangelo, a fortress where he effectively became a prisoner of Catherine's nephew and his out-of-control troops. The Pope would be needed to annul Henry and Catherine's marriage or to enforce any potential action or ruling a court may make, and whilst he was in his power Charles would be able to ensure he did not take any unfavourable actions against his aunt or his dynasty.[10]

Pope Clement VII by Sebastiano del Piombo, c.1531. (*Public Domain image, via Wikimedia Commons*)

For the time being Henry, Catherine and Anne were forced to settle into an uncomfortable threesome. Time was Catherine's friend, but it was not Henry and Anne's and each of them had to figure out what course of action to take, or if any should be taken at all. Catherine went to great lengths to separate Anne from Henry, increasingly keeping her rival in her own company and over one memorable card game told Anne that she had 'Good hap to stop at a king, but you are not like others, you will have all or none'.[11]

The king and queen were soon forced to face a crisis that put their disagreements over their marriage to one side as that summer the sweating sickness reappeared in England. Like last time they retreated with a reduced household to safety. The move didn't include Anne, who returned home to Hever Castle where she caught the dreaded illness; luckily for Henry she swiftly recovered. In a society that saw signs and God's will in everything that occurred around them, it is interesting to speculate what Catherine thought when she heard her rival had fallen ill. Did she believe it was divine retribution on Anne for her acts and behaviour? She was only human after all. Catherine was a devout woman who never questioned God's will but did a small part of her wonder what it meant when Anne recovered?

Another piece of good news was received by Henry as he learned that the Pope had agreed that Wolsey could hear the case of his marriage in England, and that he would send a Papal Legate to assist him to ensure both sides were given a fair and equal hearing. Perhaps he had heard or been made aware of

King Henry the Eighth and Anna Bullen by T. Cook after W. Hogarth *c.*1804. Catherine would often keep Anne in her company to restrict the time Henry could spend with her, sadly it did not always work. (*Public Domain image, via Wikimedia Commons*)

some underhand actions Wolsey was already engaging in? Wolsey had previously written to his representative in Rome informing him that Henry could no longer sleep with Catherine as 'certain diseases in the queen defy all remedy'. It appears Wolsey was suggesting that Catherine was suffering from an intimate illness and he wrote further stating that 'danger may ensue to the king's person by continuing in the queens chamber'. Was Wolsey implying Catherine had a contagious illness or possibly a Sexually transmitted disease (STD)? Or was he even suggesting Catherine could be violent to Henry?

The latter suggestion seems so out of character from what we know of Catherine that we can dismiss it entirely. It is more likely Wolsey was claiming that Catherine was suffering from an illness that made further sexual relations almost impossible, but was it true? Wolsey was not above lying to achieve his aims. He later falsely claimed that the bloodstained sheets from Arthur and Catherine's marriage bed were dispatched to Spain to prove the consummation of their marriage in 1501 and that Catherine was a frenzied woman with a desire for sex.

Cardinal Lorenzo Campeggio by an unknown artist, c. eighteenth century. Campeggio found himself caught between both Henry and Catherine and both wanted very different things from him. (*Public Domain image, via Wikimedia Commons*)

It is more likely Wolsey and perhaps Henry were throwing everything they could at Catherine, no matter how low they had to sink to prove the case for an annulment.[12] Things would turn nastier.

The man chosen for the unenviable task of hearing the case for and against the royal marriage was Cardinal Lorenzo Campeggio, Clement appointed him in June but he would not arrive in England until October that same year. Campeggio was riddled with gout which made travelling torture for him, but his illness was also perhaps used as a delaying tactic in the hope that one of the parties in England would have given way upon his arrival. If that is what he hoped he was to be disappointed; all three involved were as eager for his arrival as each other. He was forced to take to his bed upon his arrival in London on 8 October and it was not until 24 October that he would be able to see and speak with Catherine. But first he had to meet with the king.

Henry and Anne wanted the case heard in London, believing that a judgement would almost certainly be concluded in their favour. Catherine wanted the case to be revoked to the court in Rome for the same reason. She knew she would not get a fair hearing in England as every single churchman, lawyer and nobleman involved in the case was her husband's subject and it would take a very brave man to stand against his king's desires.

Campeggio attempted to persuade Henry against his cause of action, reminding him of the qualities of his wife and queen, but his words fell on deaf ears. As he later wrote to the Pope's secretary, Henry was so sure his marriage was invalid that 'an angel descending from heaven would be unable to persuade him otherwise'.[13] Campeggio was forced to try another angle. If he could not persuade Henry to change course, perhaps he would have more luck with Catherine?

Catherine must have been relieved upon finally coming face to face with the Papal Legate; here now was a man from Rome, independent of her husband and appointed by the Pope himself. He had been sent to ensure the proceedings moved with fairness for both parties and he would surely see why the case could not be heard in England. Her relief must have quickly turned to disappointment when she heard what he had to say. He immediately tried to persuade her of the benefits of convent life, where she could spend the rest of her life without a loss of face or dignity.[14] We can see why he suggested this course – Catherine was famous for her piety and as the daughter of Catholic monarchs it was perhaps easy for him to believe that she would come to see this is as a true vocation. Catherine, however, had been raised by her parents to believe she was destined to be the queen of England; both them and God had put her on this path and she would not stray from it.

Catherine was not naive; she was aware there was more at stake than just her marriage. The Church she belonged too was increasingly under scrutiny and attack from reformers and she herself had been at the heart of politics for over twenty years so she would not have expected an entirely altruistic solution to her difficulties. But to have her opening meeting with the Legate essentially reduced to bargaining for her future, instead of a genuine inquiry into the truth of the matter, must have been upsetting. However, Catherine kept her composure and provided a noncommittal answer.

Instead what she did was ask her husband if she could make her confession to Campeggio. Henry immediately agreed, perhaps hoping that she would say something that could be used to further his cause. The seal of the confessional was supposed to be sacrosanct between the confessor and penitent, but in high profile cases such as these it is not difficult to believe some pressure would have been brought to find out what the queen had said. Catherine, however, gave Campeggio permission herself to break the seal. She had something to say and she wanted the world to be aware. If Henry had thought she would confess that her marriage to Arthur was consummated, he was soon rudely awakened.

Catherine visited Campeggio in his own lodgings at Bath Place in London and his later writings tell us exactly what she told him:

She affirmed, on her conscience, that from 14 November, when she was espoused to the late [prince] Arthur, to 2 April following, when he died, she did not sleep with him more than seven nights et che da liu resto intacta et incorrupta, come venne dal ventre di sua madre.[15]

'Et che da liu resto intacta et incorrupta, come venne dal ventre di sua madre' translates to 'and from him it remains intact and incorrupt, as it came from its mother's womb'. Catherine was telling Campeggio that she shared a bed with her husband some nights, but he did not touch her, and she remained as she had been when her mother had given birth to her.

It is a powerful statement, and one made in the sacred seal of the confessional and as such Catherine knew it would be given a lot of weight by those around her. As she had given permission for Campeggio to break the seal, she knew it would be passed onto the Pope himself.

But did she tell the truth? We know that Catherine was a devout woman who held fast to her faith and firmly believed God had put her on her path to be queen of England, but now she was facing the loss of her marriage, her child's legitimacy and rights and an attack on her Church. Might she have thought that it was worth the risk to tell a small lie for the good of many and seek to be forgiven later? We will never know for sure, and we must each decide if we believe her word.

Soon after her confession, Catherine learnt that Henry and Wolsey were focussing on a potential flaw in the bull of dispensation allowing their marriage in 1509. The dispensation's wording stated that Catherine and Arthur's marriage had 'perhaps' been consummated and Wolsey believed this invalidated the entire document and the marriage itself. Catherine, however, had an ace up her sleeve. She had recently learnt that in Spain, found amongst the papers of the Spanish ambassador from her youth, Dr de Puebla, was both the bull and a brief on the subject. The brief's wording was different to the bull and actually eliminated the difficulty caused by the word 'perhaps' and Catherine now had a copy of it

Catherine of Aragon by Lucas Horenbout, c.1525. (*Public Domain image, via Wikimedia Commons*)

in her own papers.[16] This brief had been sent to Catherine's mother to comfort her in her final days[17] when perhaps the wording of the original bull had played on her own mind.

Henry and Wolsey were entirely unaware of the existence of this brief and furiously ordered a search of the English royal archives for their own copy. When none was found, they claimed the Spanish brief was a forgery and demanded that Catherine write to her nephew and have the original sent to them. Catherine dutifully complied but secretly sent her physician with a separate message asking Charles to keep hold if it; she had concerns that once it reached England it would 'disappear'. Charles agreed entirely with his aunt and would never allow the brief to leave Spain, sending only a notarised copy to Henry and Wolsey.

Whilst the Spanish brief removed a part of Henry and Wolsey's case against her, it also damaged Catherine as it stated her marriage to Arthur HAD been consummated. So she took an oath on the subject of her virginity to remove any doubts. Catherine swore in the presence of leading churchmen 'that she does not admit those words inserted in the brief' (her marriage to Arthur was consummated). She held the Holy Gospel in her hand and continued to say that such words were 'lacking any decree or knowledge'.[18]

All options for negotiation had failed; an inquiry was now inevitable.

On 31 May 1529, Wolsey and Campeggio opened the Legatine Court at Blackfriars and sat to judge the royal marriage. The day after both Henry and Catherine received summons to attend from the Bishop of Bath and Wells, John Clerk, and the Bishop of Lincoln, John Longland. It was a completely unprecedented event in English history and Catherine marvelled at receiving the summons, asking the surely uncomfortable Bishops why nothing had been raised in the last twenty years? During that time she had met many learned men and not one had questioned her position before. On 16 and 18 June, Catherine protested the legality of the court both verbally and in writing, before showing the court her written appeal to the Pope. She maintained her argument that both Wolsey and Campeggio were disqualified from hearing her case because of their close association with Henry. A little-known fact is that Campeggio had previously visited England in 1518 and had so impressed Henry that he bestowed on him the Bishopric of Salisbury, which he held until 1534.[19] Catherine demanded, quite reasonably, that her case be heard by impartial judges; her appeal was rejected.

Henry and Catherine attended on 21 June and sat opposite each other on either side of the hall. Henry sat on a chair made of rich tissue beneath a cloth of estate, whilst Catherine's was described as simply a rich chair. Catherine was forced to listen to Henry's lies as he spoke, first telling the court that he had felt from the beginning that there may be something wrong with his marriage but he

The Court for the Trial of Queen Katherine by George Henry Harlow, c.1817. An interpretation of the events at the Legatine Court at Blackfriars. (*Public Domain image, via Wikimedia Commons*)

had not raised it sooner for 'great love he had, and had, for her'. He then went on to claim that he desired 'more than anything else, that the marriage should be declared valid'.

Henry argued against the case being heard in Rome. His reasoning was the same reason Catherine did not want it heard in England – he did not believe he would receive a fair hearing considering Charles' power there. He stated that Catherine had had her choice of prelates and lawyers to advise and council her. Catherines advisors were primarily led by John Fisher, Bishop of Rochester and John Clerk, Bishop of Bath and Wells.[20]

Despite Catherine's concerns, Fisher would be one of the most determined advocates for her cause. A man of principle,

John Fisher, Bishop of Rochester by Hans Holbein the Younger, c.1532–35. (*Public Domain image, via Wikimedia Commons*)

Henry VIII and Catherine of Aragon before Papal Legates at Blackfriars, 1529 by Frank O'Salisbury, c.1910. Kneeling before her husband in front of high ranking members of the Church and other courtiers and witnesses, Catherine gave the speech of her life. (*CC 4.0; Public Domain image, via Wikimedia Commons*)

he was committed to finding the truth of the matter and once convinced of Catherine's cause, could not be persuaded away from his principles, not even to serve his king. He would publicly contradict Henry when he claimed he had the backing of his bishops[21] and stated that he had a document signed with seals to that effect. Fisher flatly denied he had ever signed such a document, leaving an embarrassed Henry to bluster that he was only one man.

It was now Catherine's turn to speak. She calmly stood but instead of speaking she crossed the floor of the hall to her husband, where she knelt before him and gave the speech of her life[22]:

Sir, I beseech you for all the loves that hath been between us, and for the love of God, let me have justice and right, take of me some pity and compassion, for I am a poor woman and a stranger born out of your dominion, I have here no assured friend, and much less indifferent counsel: I flee to you as to the head of justice within this realm.

Alas! Sir, wherein have I offended you, or what occasion of displeasure have I designed against your will and pleasure? Intending (as I perceive) to put me from you, I take God and all the world to witness, that I have been to you a true and humble wife, ever conformable to your will and pleasure, that never said or did anything to the contrary thereof, being always well pleased and contented with all things wherein ye had any delight or dalliance, whether it were in little or much, I never grudged in word or countenance, or showed a visage or spark of discontentation. I loved all those whom ye loved only for your sake, whether I had cause or no; and whether they were my friends or my enemies.

This twenty years I have been your true wife or more, and by me ye have had divers children, although it hath pleased God to call them out of this world, which hath been no default in me.

And when ye had me at the first, I take God to be my judge, I was a true maid without touch of man. And whether it be true or no, I put it to your conscience. If there be any just cause by the law that ye can allege against me, either of dishonesty or any other impediment to banish and put me from you, I am well content to depart, to my great shame and dishonor, and if there be none, then here I most lowly beseech you let me remain in my former estate, and receive justice at your princely hand.

The king, your father, was in the time of his reign of such estimation through the world for his excellent wisdom, that he was accounted and called of all men the second Solomon; and my father Ferdinand, King of Spain, who was esteemed to be one of the wittiest princes that reigned in Spain many years before, were both wise and excellent kings in wisdom and princely behaviour. It is not therefore to be doubted, but that they were elected and gathered as wise counsellors about them as to their high discretions was thought meet.

Also, as me seemeth there was in those days as wise, as well-learned men, and men of good judgement as be present in both realms, who thought then the marriage between you and me good and lawful. Therefore, is it a wonder to me what new inventions are now invented against me, that never intended but honesty. And cause me to stand to the order and judgment of this new court, wherein ye may do me much wrong, if ye intend any cruelty; for ye may condemn me for lack of sufficient answer, having no indifferent counsel, but such as be assigned me, with whose wisdom and learning I am not acquainted. Ye must consider that they cannot be indifferent counsellors for my part which be your subjects, and taken out of your own council before, wherein they be made privy, and dare not, for your displeasure, disobey your will and intent, being once made privy thereto.

Therefore, I most humbly require you, in the way of charity, and for the love of God, who is the just judge, to spare the extremity of this new court, until I may be advertised what way and order my friends in Spain will advise me to take. And if ye will not extend to me so much indifferent favour, your pleasure then be fulfilled, and to God I commit my case![23]

Twice during her speech, Henry attempted to raise Catherine but failed. It was only when she had finished speaking that she stood, curtseyed to her husband and turned to walk out of the court on the arm of her receiver general, Master Griffith. The court crier attempted to stop her shouting 'Catherine Queen of England, come into the Court' but Catherine walked on, telling Griffith 'On, on it maketh no matter, for it is no indifferent court for me, therefore I will not tarry; go on your ways'.

Once she had departed, Henry admitted she had 'been to me as true, as obedient, and as conformable a wife as I could in my fantasy wish or desire.

The Trial of Queen Catherine of Aragon by Henry Nelson O'Neil *c.* nineteenth century. Catherine was not just fighting for her marriage but her daughter's rights and her beloved Church. (*Public Domain image, via Wikimedia Commons*)

She hath all the virtuous qualities that ought to be in a woman of her dignity, she is also a noble woman born'. However, he continued 'all such male issue as I have received of the queen died incontinent after they were born, so that I doubt the punishment of God in that behalf'. Henry told the court he wished to 'take another wife in case that my first copulation with this gentlewoman were not lawful, which I intend not for any carnal concupiscence, ne for any displeasure or mislike of the queens person or age, with whom I could be as well content to continue during my life, if our marriage may stand with God's laws as with any woman alive'.[24]

On 25 June, Henry put forward twelve articles against his marriage to Catherine; some of the articles would have been familiar to the court but one such referred to another event that apparently occurred in 1509. Supposedly there had been 'a grave, immense and widespread scandal amongst the clergy and the people of England and in other places concerning such a marriage and that obloquy and insistent murmuring against it arose amongst the nations'.[25] This was another blatant lie; there was no general murmurings against Henry and Catherine's marriage and the only person recorded to have raised a query about it had been easily persuaded otherwise. The people of England had taken Catherine to their hearts upon their first glimpse of her and she would never leave them. The only murmurings against the king and queen's marriage originated from Henry himself and they were not always for the reasons his insisted on.

The inquiry would drag on for another month achieving nothing, but Catherine would never return to witness its failure. She had said what she had to say and that was that. Fisher argued strongly in her absence for her, quoting scripture and returning to Catherine's sworn statements of virginity each time a discussion of the potential consummation of her marriage to Arthur arose. Fisher was an educated man who had later become a Doctor of Theology and he firmly believed that only God could break apart this marriage. Wolsey desperately tried to bring in surviving testimony from those who had been there on Arthur and Catherine's wedding night but their statements consisted of them universally agreeing the couple were put to bed together and yes, they were of age to have consummated their marriage, but no one had been in the bedchamber with them to witness the act take place. Suffolk recalled the prince boasting the day after his wedding night that he had been 'in the midst of Spain' but again this could not be proven either way. In July, Wolsey and Campeggio visited Catherine in her chambers again, once more attempting to entreat her to enter a convent of her choice and settle the matter that way. She responded to a surely despairing Wolsey:

Katherine of Aragon Denounced Before King Henry VIII and His Council by Laslett John Pott, c.1880. (*Public Domain image, via Wikimedia Commons*)

> *I am a poor woman lacking both wit and understanding sufficiently to answer such approved wise men as ye be both, in so weighty a matter. I am a simple woman, destitute and barren of friendship and counsel here in a foreign region.*

She had greeted them with white thread around her neck and claimed she had been busy sewing with her ladies when they interrupted her and had barely been giving any weighty matters a thought.[26]

The Legatine Court was finally suspended by the Pope on 13 July; the news reached London on 22nd. At the end of the month, Campeggio publicly announced the suspension on the pretext that papal business was traditionally suspended over the summer and stated it would reconvene on 1 October – it never did. Just over a month later, on 1 September, the case was referred back to Rome.

To ensure nothing like this happened again, Catherine wrote to the Imperial ambassador, John Antony Musettula, and asked him to petition the Pope on her behalf that this matter never be reopened. She wanted the Pope to impose on her husband 'perpetual silence, or at least to commit the judgement to Cardinals at the court of Rome, or papal auditors'. The petition went further asking the Pope to 'forbid anything to be done prejudicial to the cause' or to allow a new 'marriage to be contracted by the King under the penalties of ecclesiastical censure, to be assisted by the secular arm if need be'.[27] Whilst it's unclear if Catherine herself wrote this last part, as the secular arm refers to the legal authority of the civil power invoked by the Church to punish offenders, we know she was certainly not afraid of a fight or a war in the physical sense. But Catherine would later be notoriously reluctant to wage physical war on her husband, the man she still loved. At this time, it is more likely Musettula was adding his own thoughts to her requests.

The failure of Blackfriars to reach a verdict and the revocation of the case to Rome was a victory for Catherine, but it in the long term it would prove to be a hollow one.

Did Arthur and Catherine consummate their marriage? Catherine always insisted they didn't but Arthur implied that they had; however could they both have been right? It has been hypothesised that whatever took place in their bedchamber on the first night of their marriage may have been enough for Arthur to think he HAD succeeded and consummated his marriage. Later Catherine, with the benefit of experience including two decades of marriage and several pregnancies, was able to look back on her first marriage and know it was not. At the time of their marriage, they were both inexperienced teenagers and there was no such thing as 'the talk'. This may have been what Catherine was attempting to ask about or confide in her confessor that led him to think it had been consummated? Perhaps neither Arthur nor Catherine was lying, but Arthur was just mistaken?

Chapter 8

Exile

For a time, Henry, Catherine and Anne were forced to settle into an uneasy ménage à trois. Catherine was still the queen and Henry was no closer to being free to remarry, but that did not mean they weren't busy behind the scenes. Henry had been encouraged to put the question of his marriage to the European universities and he sent agents to France and Italy to seek their opinions.

Anne was encouraging Henry to look further afield too. She had been persuaded of the need for reform within the Church whilst living in France and she brought this belief back with her to England. With the failure of Blackfriars, she felt able to bring her beliefs more into the open, and she even gave Henry a book to read that he had recently banned. Written by William Tyndale, *Obedience of a Christian Man* was a revolutionary book that stated there was

The Courtship of Anne Boleyn by Emanuel Leutze, *c.*1846. Catherine looks on as Anne and Henry grow closer. (*Public Domain image, via Wikimedia Commons*)

no higher authority than a king, not even a Pope, and that secular rulers did not owe their loyalty and obedience to him. Henry, who was frustrated with the Pope, at this time declared 'This Book is for me and all Kings to read'.[1]

Catherine also sent agents to scour Spanish universities on her behalf but had to be a lot more careful than her husband as she was being watched. Happily for Catherine, in August a man arrived in England who would prove himself a devoted friend and ally to both her and her daughter. The Spanish Ambassador to England, Inigo de Mendoza, had asked to be recalled to Spain citing poor health and his replacement was the university educated Eustace Chapuys. Chapuys had studied at the University of Turin and was a well-respected Doctor of Civil and Canon Law, making him a perfect ally for Catherine's cause. He first met Catherine face to face on 18 September 1529 but had already been receiving discreet visits from one of her messengers in his own property. Catherine was determined that her ally should be aware of all that he was about to walk into.[2] As a representative of her powerful nephew, Henry and his councillors were likely nervous of what this unknown man was capable of and what he may advise Catherine.

Contemporary portrait of Eustace Chapuys at the Musée-Château d'Annecy at Annecy, artist unknown. Chapuys would prove himself a loyal and devoted friend to Catherine. (*Public Domain image, via Wikimedia Commons*)

Interestingly, it is thanks to Chapuys that we have more evidence of Henry's thoughts on the matter of his wife's marriage to his brother. Thanks to the situation they found themselves in, tension had been steadily rising which spilt over into spats. On one occasion, when Henry had had dinner with his wife, he turned to her and said 'she wished to serve her interests and defend the validity of dispensation by claiming that Arthur had never consummated his marriage which was all well and good, but no less was our marriage illegal'. He went on to say that the bull did not cover the issue of public honesty and that he intended to pursue this. Catherine immediately countered:

> ... *whatever arguments were used to convince her that she was not his lawful and legitimate wife would be of no avail; she considered herself such. That was not the time or place to dispute about such matters, and that they had better go to Rome, and have the question determined by the Pope.*[3]

Meals would increasingly end in acrimony between the two and on 30 November, Catherine apparently snapped and gave full vent to her feelings, telling Henry that 'she had long been suffering the pains of Purgatory on earth, and that she was very badly treated by his refusing to dine with and visit her in her apartments'. Henry told her she had no reason to complain as she was the head of her own household and could do as she pleased in it and that he had been busy sorting out the mess Wolsey had left behind him. The cardinal had become the first victim of the failure of Blackfriars – he had been forced to surrender the Great Seal and leave the court for his long-neglected Bishopric in York. He would later be charged with praemunire (placing his allegiance to the Pope before his king) but fortunately for him died before he reached London, thus saving himself from perhaps a worse fate.

Catherine of Aragon by Joannes Corvus, c.1560. (*Public Domain image, via Wikimedia Commons*)

Henry told Catherine that 'as to visiting her in her apartments and partaking of her bed, she ought to know that he was not her legitimate husband, as innumerable doctors and canonists, all men of honour and probity, and even his own almoner, Doctor Lee, who had once known her in Spain were ready to maintain'. He continued that he was only waiting the results of his canvassing the Parisian universities to forward them to Rome and if the Pope did not confirm and declare the marriage null and void 'then in that case he would denounce the Pope as a heretic and marry whom he pleased'.

Henry may have hoped he could eventually browbeat his wife into submission, but he had forgotten who he had married. Catherine replied 'that the principal cause alleged for the divorce did not really exist, because she had come to him as a virgin, as he himself had owned upon more than one occasion'. She continued that she did not care about the opinion of his almoner as he was not her judge and 'for each doctor or lawyer, who might decide in your favour and against me, I shall find a 1000 to declare that the marriage is good and indissoluble'.

Henry stormed out shortly afterwards. In better times, Catherine knew, and still did know, that the best way to communicate with Henry was by persuasion and fair words, not arguments and disagreements and this is a sign of the immense pressure she was under that she momentarily lost her much respected calm and composure.[4] Henry would find no comfort with Anne either. She heard what had taken place, and if Henry appears to have forgotten who Catherine was and what she stood for, Anne certainly hadn't, telling him:

> *Did I not tell you that whenever you disputed with the Queen she was sure to have the upper hand? I see that some fine morning you will succumb to her reasoning, and that you will cast me off. I have been waiting long and might in the meanwhile have contracted some advantageous marriage, out of which I might have had issue, which is the greatest consolation in this world; but alas! Farewell to my time and youth spent to no purpose at all.*[5]

Shortly after Catherine was sent away to Richmond, supposedly out of concern for her health, and whilst this may have relieved the immediate pressure on them all, it left Catherine isolated from the man she loved and unable to fight for her marriage directly. Thankfully it was a brief separation and she would return to court by Christmas, where appearances were once again maintained by both parties.

More troubling for Catherine were the actions of parliament. The Reformation Parliament as it became known, sat for the first time on 3 November 1529 and its main objectives were the removal of Wolsey and the reform of ecclesiastical abuses. There is no dispute that there was some corruption involving the use of Church funds and bribery and abuses such as the holding of multiple offices and engaging in trade, and one of the key steps was to stop the trial of crimes committed by holy men in the Church's own ecclesiastical courts. These courts had seen men of God let off for heinous crimes and had been a bone of contention long before Henry's reign. Now holy men who committed crimes would be brought before a secular court. That was not all, this parliament would lay the groundwork and legislation for the break with Rome, though none knew it yet. A big step was taken in February 1530 when the clergy were compelled to recognise Henry as Head of the Church in England, thereby displacing the Pope, to the horror of Rome and traditional Catholics around Europe.[6]

There was a very real possibility war could have broken out over Henry's course of action, not just for his actions against the Church but his determination to set Catherine aside and marry Anne. The latter led to the public's sympathy very much lying with Catherine as the wronged wife and for her nephew, Charles, Henry's actions were a personal, political and religious affront. He wrote to his brother that he was contemplating going to war on their aunt and the Pope's behalf and stated he had around 20,000 men prepared. Henry would always

Empress Isabella of Portugal by Titian, *c.*1548. Catherine's niece through her sister Maria, Charles V married Isabella instead of Catherine's daughter, but she would turn to them both in her time of need. (*Public Domain image, via Wikimedia Commons*)

watch Charles and Rome's action or inaction with some nervousness, though he would never admit so in public where he kept up his usually brave and outspoken bravado. It was largely down to timing, resources, luck and Catherine herself that there was never a war, not any skill or diplomacy on Henry's part.

Catherine found herself being slowly evermore isolated. She was aware that Henry and his councillors had increased the watch on the people who came and went from her apartments. When Chapuys attempted to pay her a visit, with Henry's permission, Anne's father, now the Earl of Wiltshire, was commanded to go with him and attempted to talk him out of it, claiming Catherine was not there and had gone to hear a sermon. Chapuys insisted on visiting her and found Catherine sitting quietly in her chamber. She was still able to get letters to her supporters but she had to be discreet. She didn't just write to Charles pleading for assistance, but his wife the Empress Isabella, his sister and her niece Maria, Queen of Hungary and her sister-in-law, Margaret too.

Heartbreakingly for Catherine, she saw less of her daughter as Henry was keeping the two apart as punishment for Catherine's defiant behaviour, and she also found herself living separately from Henry more and more. Whilst they were under the same roof at Windsor, another confrontation took place in June when Catherine had a private audience with her husband. She was not thinking of just herself and her husband with her words but also the welfare of her country, and she pleaded with him to:

> … *be again to her a good prince and husband, and to quit the evil life he was leading and the bad example he was setting, and that even if he would shew no regard for her, who was, as he well knew, his true and lawful wife, that he should at least respect God and his conscience.*[7]

When she told him that he could not ignore the words of the Pope in forbidding him to remarry, Henry simply responded that the Pope did as the Emperor told him to and walked out on her. This disagreement was shortly followed by another involving a mundane everyday occurrence, Henry was once again trying to have his cake and eat it, as despite the fact he was maintaining that Catherine was not his lawful wife he still asked her to make his shirts, a duty Catherine had happily fulfilled throughout their entire marriage. Anne became aware of this and sent for the gentleman whom Henry had sent to Catherine with the cloth and berated him in the king's presence; this despite Henry truthfully stating the gentleman had only been acting on his commands. Sewing a husband's shirt was considered a wife's duty and even Catherine's mother had set time aside to perform the same duty for her father.

By July 1530, the results of the universities had started trickling back to England. It appeared that the University of Paris had found in favour of the king though the verdict would soon prove controversial. Accusations of bribery and corruption would not be misplaced here as it was later proven that 100 doctors had voted in favour of the King but 44 had actually voted in favour of Catherine, and this had then been covered up.

Close up of the arms of Queen Catherine of Aragon alongside the Tudor rose at Christchurch Gate at Canterbury Cathedral. (*Attribution LBM1948, Wikimedia, CC 3.0; Public Domain image, via Wikimedia Commons*)

A year later, both Catherine and Henry were aware that the universities of Salamanca and Alcala had found in favour of Catherine, but a controversial pamphlet titled 'The Determinations of the Most Famous and Most Excellent Universities of Italy and France, that it is so Unlawful for a Man to Marry his Brothers wife, that the Pope hath no power to dispense therewith' revealed that Henry had won the argument. Fifty-three universities ruled the marriage was unlawful whilst forty-two disagreed and five claimed they were unsure but ruled the Church would uphold the marriage, leaving a margin of six. This was not as devastating to Catherine as it sounded as it was later revealed that in fact only two or three doctors voted.

Henry made one final attempt to browbeat Catherine into submission, sending a delegation of noblemen and clergy to his wife in her own chambers late at night to demand she submit to her husband's wishes. The usual claims were made – that she had been Arthur's wife and their marriage had been consummated but the Duke of Norfolk went further telling her she had humiliated her husband by attempting to have him summoned to Rome and demanded that she agree to her case being heard in England. He went on to say that England had provided much assistance to her father and her nephew over the years and she had been treated honourably as England's Queen; she had no cause to complain he reasoned.

As Henry had, his men clearly forgot who they were dealing with as Catherine once again calmly rose to the occasion and responded that she was Henry's lawful wife and that she would not consent to the matter being heard in England and would only accept judgement from the Pope.

When Henrys almoner, Dr Lee, attempted to accuse her of having slept with Arthur, thereby implying she was a liar, she cut him down to size, telling him he was more interested in flattering the king than the truth of the matter. His colleague, Dr Sampson, fared no better when he breezily stated she may as well give up as any papal verdict would be overturned. Catherine replied to him that he had no idea of what she had suffered since the proceedings began. The final insult came from Bishop John Longland who told her that she must have been living in sin with Henry as God had punished them by the loss of their children.[8]

King Henry VIII by Hans Holbein the Younger, *c.*1537. Henry left Catherine at Windsor and did not even give her the courtesy of a goodbye. (*Public Domain image, via Wikimedia Commons*)

How Catherine felt upon hearing these disgusting words can only be imagined, but she kept her composure and calmly stated she was the king's lawful wife and dismissed them, saying it seemed strange that so many honourable men of power and influence were required to call on a poor, friendless and defenceless woman. She told them to take a message back to her husband. She stated that she would obey him in everything save for those which touched her two greater allegiances: God and her conscience.

In July, whilst the court was at Windsor, Henry and Anne rode to Woodstock leaving Catherine behind. She would never see her husband again.

Catherine did not realise Henry had left her at first, it was only at the end of the month when she sent after him to enquire after his health that she was rudely awakened. Henry was furious upon receiving her message and dispatched his own messenger to tell her that he had:

> ... *no need to bid her adieu, nor to give her that consolation of which she spoke, nor any other, and still less that she should send to visit him, or to inquire of his*

estate; that she had given him occasion to speak such things, and that he was sorry and angry at her because she had wished to bring shame upon him by having him personally cited; and still more, she had refused (like an obstinate woman she was) the just and reasonable request made by his Council and other nobles of his realm; that she had done all this in trust of Your Majesty [the Emperor], but she ought to consider that God was more powerful than you; and, for a conclusion, that henceforth she must desist from sending him messengers and visitors.

Catherine did not take the rejection lying down, replying that she was sorry for the 'anger and ill will he had against her without cause for she had done everything for the honour and discharge of their consciences'. She continued, 'her hope did not depend upon his majesty, nor on any prince alive, but only on God, who was the real protector of truth and justice'. It took Henry three days to reply to her – when he did, it was another round of the same arguments they had both been maintaining: he stated she was obstinate to claim she had never known Prince Arthur and that he would prove otherwise and that she should best use her time to find witnesses to prove her supposed virginity.[9]

Despite what had just happened, Catherine was able to have her daughter visit her at Windsor, and this must have cheered her. They spent their time together hunting and riding, but this would cruelly be another last for Catherine as well – after this visit she would never see her daughter again either. In the middle of August, Catherine was commanded to leave Windsor and travel to The More; Mary was to go to Richmond. Catherine did not like The More,

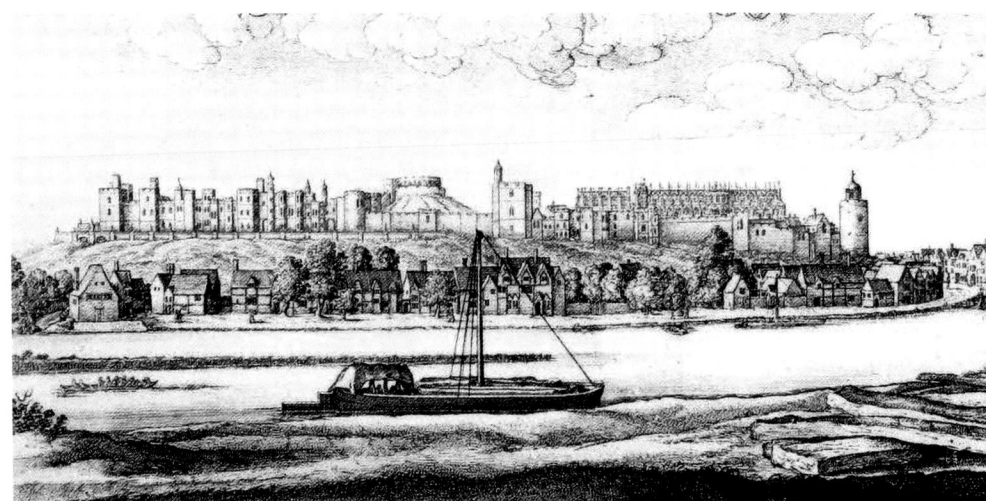

Windsor Castle in 1672, seen from the river, by Wenceslaus Hollar. Henry left Catherine behind at Windsor and it was here that she would see her daughter for the last time as well. (*Public Domain image, via Wikimedia Commons*)

calling it 'one of the worst houses in England' though it's not clear as to why she thought this; it may have been more that she objected to being removed from the heart of events. She later told Chapuys she would have preferred to have been sent to the Tower because then at least everyone would have been aware of her misfortune and 'would pray God to give her patience, and inspire the king to treat her better'.[10] Apart from separation from the people she loved, no other move was made against Catherine at this time; she still retained her large household and was served and treated as queen.

At The More, a softer approach was attempted to persuade Catherine to change her mind. Drs Lee and Sampson were sent to her, this time with the Earl of Sussex, but again Catherine politely

Engraving of Queen Catherine of Aragon from *Biographical Sketches of the Queens of England*, engraved by W. H. Mote after an illustration by J. W. Wright, c. nineteenth century. (*Public Domain image, via Wikimedia Commons*)

refused, although this time she made a slightly different response. She now told them that she had originally believed Henry was acting according to a scruple of his conscience but had now realised he was motivated 'by mere passion, so she would not be so ill advised as to consent to the compromise which the king required, especially here, where everybody, either for fear or subornment, would say black was white, and that the king ought not to doubt that she would pursue the process commenced by him, seeing that she had done everything by his leave'.

At this point all three men fell to their knees before her, begging her for the honour of the king, the princess, the peace of the kingdom and her own peace of mind to allow the process to be decided in England. Catherine, not to be outdone, fell to her own knees 'praying them for the honour of God and his Passion, for discharge of the King's conscience and her own, to remove such a scandalous example from Christendom for the good and peace of the realm'. She implored them to persuade the king to return to her 'as he knew that she was his true and lawful wife; or, if he had any scruple, he would allow it to be cleared at Rome, where it could not be supposed that your Majesty had employed any violence or practice, for you were a very just prince'.[11] As they probably expected, the men were forced to return to Henry empty handed.

After this, Catherine and Henry would almost meet one final time when they both attended a feast for the Serjeant-at-arms at Ely House in November, but Henry commanded that Catherine dine separately from him and so they never encountered each other. Catherine wrote a letter shortly after this sad experience:

> *My tribulations are so great, my life so disturbed by the plans daily invented to further the kings wicked intention, the surprises which the king gives me, which certain persons of his Council, are so mortal, and my treatment is what God knows, that it is enough to shorten ten lives, much more mine. As far as concerns this business, I have offended neither God nor the King, to whom I have always shown obedience as a true wife, and sometimes more so in this affair than my conscience approved of. Yet they treat me in such a manner that I do not know what to do, except to complain to God and your Majesty, with whom my remedy lies, and to beg you to cause the Pope to make such a speedy end of the matter as my truth merits. I pray God to pardon the Pope for his delay. In this world I will confess myself to be the king's true wife, and in the next they will know how unreasonably I am afflicted.*[12]

Christmas came and Catherine did not receive a present from Henry; in fact a record of gifts shows that the space next to the queen's name is blank. Catherine did not send one to him as she had been forbidden too, but she found a loophole. Henry had ordered her not to send him a Christmas present but he had not banned her from doing so for the New Year. Catherine chose to send him a gold cup but someone was able to intercept it, so it was never officially presented to Henry who became aware of the gift later. Whilst he admired the handiwork, he returned it to Catherine stating as they were not married it was no longer appropriate for her to send him gifts.

1532 would continue to bode ill for Catherine. On 15 May, the clergy finally submitted to Henry, though it would not be until 1534 that the Submission of the Clergy and Restraint of Appeals Act would officially pass in parliament. By their submission the clergy agreed to give up their power to formulate laws without the king's licence and assent. Henry was now effectively the Head of the Church in England and there was now no recourse to the Pope in Rome. With Catherine cut off from events, we can't be sure when she discovered this but as she continued to appeal to the Pope, we can deduce what she thought of the Act. The same month she was forced to move to Hatfield, in Hertfordshire, but still no change was made to her status, though it was obvious to everyone that her title of queen was looking increasingly empty. It was Anne Boleyn who appeared at Henry's side, magnificently dressed and able to acquire favours and intercede with him on others' behalf.

Catherine still retained her popularity with the English people, much to Henry and Anne's annoyance. Her chaplain, Thomas Abel, took a risk when he published a book in her defence called *Invicta Veritas* (Invincible Truth), which landed him a spell in the Tower whilst his work was suppressed. He was held in the Beauchamp Tower where today graffiti can still be found depicting his name above a bell with an 'A' on the side. He would not be so fortunate a few years later. John Fisher and other clergyman of his opinion continued to preach in her favour, despite the dangers. Anne meanwhile was still perceived to be the person responsible for all the changes and injuries done to Catherine and she was insulted in public whenever she hunted with the king but Anne, whilst not yet queen, was having her moments of triumph.

On 1 September she was created the Marquess of Pembroke in her own right in preparation for an overseas trip she was about to make to the French court as Henry's intended wife and queen. Henry and Anne were looking for Francis' support for their marriage and Henry's actions, knowing that when they took the final step there would likely be repercussions despite their public bravado. To ensure she looked the part, Anne would need the jewels Catherine still held and so the Duke of Norfolk was dispatched to retrieve them. Catherine flatly refused to 'give up my jewels for such a wicked purpose as that of ornamenting a person who is the scandal of Christendom'[13] but conceded she would if commanded to by the king. Henry promptly did so and Catherine was forced to relinquish them. Around the time of their departure, Catherine was forced to move again to a property at Enfield, where she worried that Henry would marry Anne in France and return with her as his queen. She would have been relieved to know that this never happened, but it would be a fleeting relief as both Henry and Anne wanted their marriage to be solemnised in England, Anne especially so, as Chapuys had been informed she 'wishes it to be done here in the place where queens are wont to be married and crowned'.[14] Catherine would have been gratified to learn that no royal woman in France would receive Anne. Henry did not want to meet Francis' queen, who was Catherine's niece, Eleanor of Austria – Queen Claude having passed away; and Francis' sister also refused to meet with Anne. Francis did attempt to suggest his mistress, Anne de Pisseleu d'Heilly, Duchess d'Étampes, but she was regarded by Henry as unsuitable as Anne was to be his wife, not his mistress. In the end, the two kings met without any ladies present in Boulogne, before Henry escorted Francis to meet Anne at Calais.

After what appears to have been a successful visit, from Henry and Anne's point of view at least, the couple returned to England where either on 14

November 1532 or 25 January 1533 they were quietly married. Anne finally became Henry's wife and shortly after his queen, though in the eyes of the world and certainly Catherine's, he was still married to her.[15]

If Henry and Anne married on the former date, it could have been a deliberate reminder to Catherine of her place: Arthur and Catherine had been married on 14 November 1501.

When did Catherine learn of her husband's new marriage? She was officially made aware of it on 9 April by the Dukes of Norfolk and Suffolk, who had travelled to her residence at Ampthill Castle in Bedfordshire to plead with her to give up the case for Rome and allow it to be heard in England. Upon hearing her refusal, she was told by the two men that Henry had already remarried anyway.

Thomas Cranmer by an unknown artist, year unknown. As Archbishop of Canterbury, Cranmer would annul Catherine's marriage, though she never recognised his ability to do so, nor his verdict. (*Public Domain image, via Wikimedia Commons*)

Catherine had received a summons to attend a new court in May at Dunstable Priory by the new Archbishop of Canterbury, Thomas Cranmer – William Warham having died in August 1532 – but she ignored it. Cranmer, who had been promoted by the Boleyns and Henry, had immediately found her marriage to be null and void[16] and at the same time found Henry and Anne's to be 'good and valid'.

The blows kept coming. On 25 June, her sister-in-law and one of her oldest friends, Mary, Queen of France died. Mary had publicly sided with Catherine and refused to recognise Anne as Henry's wife and queen, creating a distance between herself and her brother, Mary's death was not just a personal loss for Catherine, but the loss of a valuable ally. Whilst Mary had retreated from the court in the years following her second marriage, she was still Henry's favourite sister and may have been able to influence her wayward brother, but now the possibility was gone forever.

On 3 July, Catherine's chamberlain, Lord William Mountjoy, in what must have been the most awkward announcement of his life, was forced to tell her that Anne had been crowned queen a month earlier. In what can only be described as a petty act, Anne's chamberlain, Sir Thomas Burgh, specifically selected Catherine's former barge for Anne's coronation and had Catherine's arms defaced. Strangely this seems to have been a step too far for Henry, who chastised the over eager Burgh and rightly pointed out that there were other barges that were fit for Anne's use.[17]

Mountjoy told Catherine that as she was no longer queen, she must content herself with the title princess dowager – the title she had held upon the death of Prince Arthur. Catherine insisted she was the queen and that she wouldn't acknowledge anyone who didn't refer to her as such. Later, when presented with a document recording an interview she had had with some of Henry's councillors in which they referred to her as the princess dowager, she scribbled out each mention of the hated title, one time so vehemently she tore the page.[18]

Many attempts would be made by Henry and his councillors to make Catherine conform, and none would be successful. Catherine was told that Henry may be forced to withdraw his affection from their daughter, that her actions could have consequences for her daughter and those servants that remained loyal to her, and that her goods would be confiscated. Later there would be vague threats of imprisonment, but each time Catherine refused to be intimidated. After one confrontation she stated:

Neither for her daughter, family possessions or any worldly adversity or displeasure that might ensue, she would yield in this cause, to put her soul in danger.

She maintained that she was 'the king's true wife and would never call herself otherwise than Queen'. When she was later accused of vainglory in wanting to keep the title of queen, she angrily denied this responding, 'she would rather be a poor beggar's wife, and be sure of Heaven, than to be Queen of all the world'. Another time she called on those attempting to intimidate her to remember her heritage:

… she would be much more proud to be called the daughter of her father and mother than to be the greatest queen in the world, if she could not conscientiously use the title.[19]

But perhaps even worse for Catherine was that Anne Boleyn had fallen pregnant as soon as she was married. Catherine's last pregnancy had ended in sadness in 1518 and she will have waited anxiously to hear the outcome; in the meantime she was forced to deal with evermore slights and humiliations. Members of her household were continuously ordered to force her to recognise her new title and state. Henry, via her servants, told her that if she would submit to him he would treat her well, otherwise 'he would punish her as his subject' and if she persevered in this obstinacy she would 'create parties in the kingdom, and confusion in the succession'. He then directly threatened their daughter, a move that confirms to us today that Henry's actions were not all at Anne's behest, even if she may have approved them. Catherine was told that 'the king would ill-treat the princess, and those who spoke of it, and all her other servants would incur the king's indignation'.

Of course, the argument that could easily be made is that it was Henry's own actions that had led to this point, but Henry could never admit to himself that he was at fault. Catherine was clearly aware of this on some level though she did not (or could not) in her response put the blame on Henry. Instead, she replied:

> *... she had perfect confidence that He who in a moment converted St Paul, and turned him from a persecutor to a preacher, would inspire the king's conscience, and not permit such a virtuous prince long to continue in error, to the slander of Christendom and ecclesiastical authority. As to the division of the kingdom, and the confusion of the succession, those only were to blame who had persuaded this new marriage, because the king had already lawful succession acknowledged by the whole kingdom; and from such an abominable marriage there could only arise a perverse offspring, which would throw all into confusion that allowed it to reign.*

As for her daughter and her servants, she continued:

> *... the king being her father could do what he pleased. No doubt she would be sorry to see her ill-treated, and also that her servants should incur the king's indignation; but neither for that, nor for any death, would she damn her soul or that of her husband the king.*[20]

In July, Catherine was moved from Ampthill to Buckden House in Cambridgeshire. This move revealed to her that whilst she may be isolated, she was not forgotten by her people who lined the route to greet her. Chapuys wrote that they 'begged her with hot tears to set them to work and employ them in her service, as they were ready to die for the love of her' and that they 'wished her joy, repose and prosperity and confusion to her enemies'.[21] It must have seemed to Catherine that perhaps her fortunes were changing when a messenger arrived at Buckden informing her that the Pope had belatedly ordered Henry to put away Anne within ten days on pain of excommunication, and he called upon her nephew and other Christian princes to enforce his bull. But sadly for Catherine, the time for Henry listening to the Pope had passed and his commands were ignored.

If she had hopes of the bull shocking Henry to his senses, she was disabused in August when attempts were made by Anne to get her to surrender a 'very rich triumphal cloth which she brought from Spain to wrap up her children with at baptism'. Catherine responded that 'it has not pleased God she should be so ill advised as to grant any favour in a case so horrible and abominable'[22] and thankfully the demand was never made again, though whether it was Henry who talked Anne out of her ill-conceived idea is not known. The robe was Catherine's own personal property, not English royal property, so it could not be seized in the same way her jewels had been.

On September 7, 1533, Anne gave birth, but it was not the much longed for son Henry had hoped for, but another daughter they would call Elizabeth after both of their mothers. Whilst Elizabeth's birth was not the defeat for Anne that it has been made out to be, as it proved that Anne was fertile and able to produce healthy children, it did still cause embarrassment as both mother and father had been so sure Anne would have a boy and vindicate their actions to the world. Nobody, not even Catherine, would then have been able to argue differently, but now they would have to try again and in the meantime continue their battle with Catherine.

Catherine was unwell that winter, perhaps because of the strain she had been under, but others, including Chapuys, believed attempts were being made on her life. When a great personage becomes an inconvenience, and Catherine was certainly proving herself an obstacle to Henry's wishes, rumours of illness and plots of assassination almost become mandatory. But there is evidence that there was a certain degree of belief and even hope in the rumours of illness, not least from Henry himself. Henry was apparently telling ambassadors that Catherine 'could not live long, as she was dropsical',[23] whilst Anne was reported to be planning to poison her. Charles, despite Henry's protestations to the contrary, had been made aware that his aunt was being harassed and deprived of her loyal servants, and living in less-than-ideal conditions – Ampthill not being considered a very healthy house – and so he had written to his own ambassadors to tell them to deny the reports of her illness.

But if Henry couldn't effectively strike at Catherine, he was able to start striking at her allies. In April 1534, the Holy Maid of Kent, Elizabeth Barton, was denounced and executed at Tyburn for maintaining 'the false opinion and wicked quarrel of the queen against the king'. Barton had been employed as a domestic servant when in 1525 she fell ill, possibly suffering a seizure. When she came to, she spoke of visions she had had, which soon took a religious significance. She was widely considered a prophetess, but she earned Henry's enmity when she spoke against his divorce and announced that he would lose his crown and his throne if he married Anne Boleyn. She also claimed to have seen the spot reserved for him in hell. Barton was arrested and examined twice; the second time saw her condemned and she and six of her associates were hanged and beheaded.[24] Catherine had wisely steered clear of this controversial figure, despite Barton's attempts to meet with her and offer her consolation, so no links could ever be made between the two women.

A letter survives from Catherine to her daughter from 1534, that was likely prompted by the passing of Henry's Act of Succession that recognised Elizabeth as his heir, not his elder daughter. Anyone of an appropriate age was required to swear an oath to this effect. The penalty of not doing so was the confiscation of body and goods, but the act went further stating:

Youthful portrait of Queen Mary I, daughter to Henry VIII and Catherine of Aragon by Wenceslaus Hollar, *c*.1647. Mary was in as difficult a situation as her mother — she was separated from both of her parents, declared illegitimate and forced to wait upon her half-sister in a household full of Anne Boleyn's relatives. She was also facing increasing pressure to recognise her father as Supreme Head of the Church of England. (*CC 4.0; Public Domain image, via Wikimedia Commons*)

> *… she [Anne] shall be regent and absolute governor of her children and the kingdom, and that applying the title of queen or princess to anyone except the said Anne or her daughter shall be considered high treason.*

Mary was in as difficult a situation as her mother: her own household had been disbanded and she had been (though Catherine seemingly didn't know it yet) separated from the Countess of Salisbury, despite the Countess' offer to serve her at her own expense. Mary was forced to move and wait upon her infant sister who was now the Princess Elizabeth and heiress to England in her place. Attempts were also being made to force her, like Catherine, to give up her title and recognise the new status quo, Mary, ever her mother's daughter, refused and like Catherine was facing increasing pressure and threats to make her comply.

> *Daughter, I heard such tidings today that I do perceive if it be true, the time is come that Almighty God will prove you; and I am very glad of it, for I trust He doth handle you with a good love. I beseech you agree of His pleasure with a merry heart; and be sure that, without fail, He will not suffer you to perish if*

you beware to offend Him. I pray you, good daughter, to offer yourself to Him. If any pangs come to you, shrive yourself; first make you clean; take heed of His commandments, and keep them as near as He will give you grace to do, for then you are sure armed. And if this lady [Anne Shelton] do come to you as it is spoken, if she do bring you a letter from the King, I am sure in the self same letter you shall be commanded what you shall do. Answer with few words, obeying the King, your father, in everything, save only that you will not offend God and lose your own soul; and go no further with learning and disputation in the matter. And wheresoever, and in whatsoever company you shall come, observe the King's commandments. Speak you few words and meddle nothing. I will send you two books in Latin; the one shall be De Vita Christi with a declaration of the Gospels, and the other the Epistles of St Jerome that he did write to Paul and Eustochium, and in them I trust you shall see good things. And sometimes for your recreation use your virginals or lute if you have any.

But one thing I especially desire you, for the love that you do owe unto God and unto me, to keep your heart with a chaste mind, and your body from all ill and wanton company, not thinking or desiring any husband for Christ's passion; neither determine yourself to any manner of living till this troublesome time be past. For I dare make sure that you shall see a very good end, and better than you can desire. I would God, good daughter, that you did know with how good a heart I do write this letter unto you. I never did one with a better, for I perceive very well that God loveth you. I beseech Him of His goodness to continue it, and if it fortune that you shall have nobody with you of your acquaintance, I think it best you keep your keys yourself, for howsoever it is, so shall be done as shall please them.

And now you shall begin, and by likelihood I shall follow. I set not a rush by it; for when they have done the uttermost they can, then I am sure of the amendment. I pray you, recommend me unto my good lady of Salisbury, and pray her to have a good heart, for we never come to the kingdom of Heaven but by troubles.

Daughter, whatsoever you come, take no pain to send unto me, for if I may, I will send to you.

Your loving mother,
Katharine the Queen.[25]

In July, Chapuys set off with a large escort to visit Catherine in what was as much a publicity stunt as it was his determination to visit her. Catherine had written to him asking him to visit and it seems they covertly plotted the resulting expedition between them. The publicity of Chapuys' visit would remind the English people of her plight, but it would also prove something. If Chapuys was allowed to see her, then she wasn't a prisoner. He had asked several times to visit Catherine, but each time had been fobbed off; now he would show Henry that Catherine was not forgotten by the Emperor and her natal family. Without Henry's permission though, he had to be careful, which is why the ambassador set off so conspicuously and progressed slowly on his journey to Catherine. As expected, his actions soon caught Henry's attention who dispatched one of his men who overtook him on the road, arriving at Kimbolton first. The man later met with Chapuys with a messenger from the steward and chamberlain in charge of Catherine's household, who stated they had received orders that Chapuys was to be denied entry. Whilst this proved that Catherine was being strictly guarded and plenty of witnesses were aware of what had occurred, it was not the public relations disaster it could have been for Henry if Chapuys had arrived at Kimbolton and had the door shut in his face. Catherine, herself, was delighted with what had been achieved. She wrote to Chapuys suggesting that it would be delightful if some of her countrymen could pass Kimbolton on their way home. Chapuys took the hint and whilst he set off on his returning journey, he sent his men ahead and later wrote:

Kimbolton Castle in Cambridgeshire, England from Morris's *Country Seats* (1880). Catherine's last home and where she sadly passed away, though she would not recognise much of the castle from this image. (*Public Domain image, via Wikimedia Commons*)

One of her chamber gave me to understand that, although she did not dare to declare it, he knew well she would have great pleasure if part of the company were to present themselves before the place; which they did next day, to the great consolation, as it seemed, of the ladies with the Queen, who spoke to them from the battlements and windows; and it seemed to the country people about that Messiah had come.[26]

Catherine had been moved to Kimbolton Castle in May 1534. Prior to that she had been forced into a very undignified confrontation with the Duke of Suffolk, though perhaps it was more embarrassing for him. When he arrived at Buckden to move her to another property called Somersham Palace, he was also there to take an oath from her servants. They were to acknowledge Henry as Supreme Head of the Church of England and that Catherine was no longer queen; failure to swear resulted in instant dismissal. Somersham Palace was in an even worse condition than her present house and surrounded by marshes which could affect her health, so Catherine flatly refused to go. She locked herself in her chamber and only communicated with Suffolk through a hole in the wall. Suffolk was forced into pleading with her through this gap to no avail and wrote back to Thomas Cromwell, Henry's new right-hand man, that the only way he could move her would be by force, a step he did not want to take without the full backing of the king and the council. He grew increasingly nervous when the servants of Catherine's that he had discharged departed Buckden and spread the tale of what was taking place there. Local villagers armed with pitchforks silently gathered around the property, watching for any sign of any injury done to the woman they still regarded as England's queen. One of the men removed was Thomas Abel, one of her chaplains, who was once again imprisoned in the Tower of London; this time he would not emerge.

For six days, Suffolk pleaded with Catherine who only told him he would have to break down her door to force her out. In the end, Suffolk was forced to retreat empty

Thomas Cromwell by Hans Holbein the Younger, c.1532–33. Cromwell became Henry's right-hand man following Wolsey's fall. (*Public Domain image, via Wikimedia Commons*)

handed, leaving Catherine with a much-reduced household that included her Spanish confessor, physician, apothecary and several maids to help her dress and undress. This may sound drastic, but Catherine was provided with another household that recognised her status as princess dowager and for this reason she would have nothing to do with them and regarded them as jailers rather than servants as they had all sworn not to recognise her as queen. These two 'households' would live very separate lives and barely interact with each other in future.

Suffolk had been forced to back down and this meant so had Henry. A sign that he had not completely forgot who the woman he once loved was, came from a comment he later made:

The Lady Catherine is a proud, stubborn woman of very high courage. If she took it into her head to take her daughters part, she could quite easily take the field, muster a great array and wage against me a war as fierce as any her mother Isabella ever waged in Spain.[27]

Even Thomas Cromwell could admire her tenacity:

Nature wronged her in not making her a man. But for her sex, she would have surpassed all the heroes of history.

Catherine would never wage a war against the man she still loved and regarded as her husband, but Henry did not know that, and in recognition of her status and ancestry, he could only 'bully' her so far without severe reprisals.

Catherine kept to her chambers and only left to hear Mass in the gallery. She ate and drank nothing that was not provided for her by her trusted servants, and in consequence her world became even smaller, but she was still able to receive information from the outside. She learnt that Henry had started to close the monasteries of the Observant Friars – an order that had been close to both her own and her mother's heart. Catherine's former confessor, Bishop John Forest, had been based in the Greenwich order, but since 1533 had been imprisoned at Newgate after he and his brothers came out in support of her. Catherine wrote to commiserate with him and asked him to pray for her. Despite his clearly desperate circumstances, Forest wrote back 'that he was happy to find her constant in the faith of the Church and begged her not to be conflicted on his account'.[28]

Shortly after her arrival at Kimbolton, she received the Archbishop of York, Edward Lee, and her former supporter the Bishop of Durham, Cuthbert Tunstall, who attempted to persuade her to take the oath. Predictably she refused, repeating her reasoning for doing so: she was Henry's lawful wife, their marriage had been a true one and it was a lie that she had ever consummated her marriage with Arthur and the Pope had pronounced in her favour. She wrote shortly after to Chapuys that she had been threatened with the penalties of the Act (i.e. death) and told the men that 'if there was anyone who had come to do such an execution let him come forward as she wished for nothing more'. Both Bishops backed down at this, perhaps realising they had exceeded their brief.

Catherine was not the only high-profile figure to refuse to take the oath. Her staunch supporter, Bishop John Fisher, and her friend the former chancellor, Sir Thomas More, also refused and for that both had been thrown in the Tower of London.

Chapter 9

Death of the Queen

Henry was still fighting to subdue Catherine's supporters, but perhaps he should have remembered what the Mayor of London had said upon being complained to that people had walked out of a service when asked to pray for Anne as queen: that he 'could not command hearts'.

In autumn, Pope Clement died and his successor was the more active and determined Paul III; this was good news for Catherine but not for Henry and Anne. The new Pope was determined to bring the disobedient Henry back into the Catholic Church but Henry had recently been granted (or granted himself) the title Supreme Head of the Church of England and was now moving against the monasteries in England. The process started slowly. First an assessment was made of all monastic property in England and then smaller monasteries that were unable to support themselves were closed and any funds they had were redirected to the king. This was perhaps a sensible policy, but it was the start of something greater. In the years to come, the monasteries would almost completely disappear from England's landscape, leaving only the ruins of their once vast and beautiful buildings. Perhaps fortunately, this was not something Catherine lived to see.

For Henry, the monasteries were a very visual reminder of the Pope and his now disregarded authority. Whilst there were some instances of corruption, as can be found in any large-scale organisation, the former was perhaps the main reason Henry reacted so swiftly against them. Some of the inhabitants of the monasteries also refused to swear the oath acknowledging Henry's new title and marriage, so were therefore guilty of treason. The most

Black chalk portrait of Catherine of Aragon by Devéria Achille (project for a lithograph; oval 12 x 13.7cm). This preparatory drawing for a lithograph or engraving seems to have been made freely on the basis of an engraving by Cornelis Martinus Vermeulen, after Adrien van der Werf. (*Public Domain image, via Wikimedia Commons*)

notable of these were the monks of the Carthusian Order in the City of London, known to history as the Carthusian Martyrs of London. They would face various fates, each of them equally horrible. The first to die was the Carthusian Prior, John Houghton, and two of his brothers, Robert Lawrence and Augustine Webster, who faced the terrible death of hanging drawing and quartering on 4 May 1535. Before he was executed, the Prior was said to have declared his fidelity to the Catholic Church and forgiven his executioners. Two more would be executed on 19 June and the fate of these men can be found in the Letters and Papers:

In 1535 eighteen of the Charterhouse were condemned for defending the liberty of the Church. Seven of them, viz., John Houghton, Robt. Lawrence, Austen Webster, Humfrey Middellmore, Wm. Exmeu, Sebastian Newdegate, and Wm. Horne, were drawn on hurdles through the city of London to the open place of execution, and there hanged, quartered, &c. Three of them, Humfrey, William, and Sebastian, had stood in prison upright, chained from their necks to their arms, and their legs fettered with locks and chains for 13 days. Their quarters were hanged on the gates and walls of the city and on the gate of the Charterhouse. Two of the eighteen, John Rochester and James Walwercke, remained hanging. The other nine died in prison with stink and miserably smothered, 'the which were these that follow'.[1]

These men would be recognised by the Catholic Church as martyrs. Just days later, on 22 June, John Fisher would be executed by beheading on Tower Green. Pope Paul III had nominated him a cardinal in December 1534, and confirmed the appointment in May 1535, perhaps thinking Henry would never move against such a high ranking man of the Church, but Henry was reported to have replied viciously that 'the Pope could send him the red hat whenever he liked, but that he would make sure that by the time it arrived he would have to wear it on his shoulder, for head he shall not have to set it on'.[2]

Pope Paul III by Titian, c.1543. A man of sterner character than his predecessor, but despite his attempts he was still unable to halt England's break with Rome or change Henry's mind. (*Public Domain image, via Wikimedia Commons*)

On 6 July, Sir Thomas More was also beheaded, but on Tower Hill. More had made every attempt to keep his conscience clear and remain loyal to his king, but it was well known he did not agree with the king's actions and had wisely chosen to keep silent in the hope that this would be enough for the king. But Henry demanded full and unconditional support from those around him, even those that had resigned their duties, retired from the court and held off from commenting on politically sensitive actions. On the scaffold, More's final words were reportedly: 'I die the King's good servant, and God's first'.[3]

The devastation Catherine felt upon hearing about these deaths cannot be imagined. Both men had been known to her and Henry, and both had been considered close friends at one time. She may also have a felt a degree of guilt that they had died refusing to acknowledge the king's title and marriage and essentially maintaining her cause, but as she had done, both men had put their beliefs first and stood by them to the end. Catherine continued to write to her family abroad asking them to intercede with the Pope and Henry on her behalf and she did not just rely on others, but petitioned the Pope directly herself as this letter reveals:

> *Has forborne to write to his Holiness as her letters are full of complaints, although not without scruple, as matters in this kingdom require greater diligence. For one thing, however, she gives thanks to Christ for having given Christendom such a vicar in a time of so great necessity. Begs him to have special consideration for this kingdom, for the King her husband, and her daughter; for, if a remedy be not applied with all speed, there will be no end to the loss of souls or to the making of martyrs. The good will be constant and suffer, the lukewarm perhaps fall away, and the rest stray like sheep without a shepherd. Writes to his Holiness plainly for discharge of her conscience as one who expects death along with her daughter. Has some comfort to think she will follow those holy men in their sufferings, though she grieves that she cannot imitate their lives. Kimbolton, 10 Oct. 1535.*[4]

Catherine may have been expecting death, but as can inferred here it was for her stance on her marriage, her daughter's rights and Henry's actions against the Church. But, instead, at sometime between 10 October and 11 December, Catherine fell ill. At this point there were no fears for her life, but she was clearly ill enough for someone to inform Cromwell. Chapuys himself had not even heard about it, when he was informed by the man himself as he revealed in a letter dated 13 December to the Emperor:

> *Having gone two days ago to see Cromwell, both to solicit payment of the Queen's arrears and to learn news, Cromwell told me he had just despatched a man to*

inform the King of the Queen's illness, who was very sick. This was the first news I had heard of it. I asked leave to go and see her. He immediately gave me leave to send one of my servants, and thereupon despatched letters; but as to my going myself he would speak to the King, whose intention he would report at his return from Court: but he has never since spoken of it, nor have I to him, because, thank God, she has recovered, and is now well. As I was leaving Cromwell I received a letter from the Queen's physician, saying that, with God's help, her illness would be nothing at all, and that if he did not notify to me that she was worse I need not be very urgent for the said licence; which I shall take care not to be.[5]

Catherine of Aragon by an unknown artist, c.1516. (*Public Domain image, via Wikimedia Commons*)

It would soon be clear that this had been a false hope and that actually Catherine was suffering her last illness. By Christmas she had worsened and her own physician, John de la Sa, wrote to Chapuys begging him to visit her as she was asking to see him. Chapuys immediately asked for permission to visit her from Henry and Cromwell, setting down his efforts in another letter to his master which disturbingly reveals Henry's priorities at this time:

At last he [Henry] said that he believed the Queen, whom he only called Madame, would not live long (ne la feroit ycy longuement), and that if she died you would have no cause to trouble yourself about the affairs of this kingdom, and might refrain from stirring in this matter (et se pourra tenir par le bec des poursuites faictes en ce negoce). I said the death of the Queen could do no possible good, and that in any event the sentence was necessary.

After I had taken leave of the King he recalled me by the duke of Suffolk to tell me news had just come that the Queen was in extremis, and that I should hardly find her alive; moreover, that this would take away all the difficulties between your Majesty and him. I think the danger cannot be so great, because the physician did not represent the case to me as so urgent; nevertheless I took horse at once. I asked leave that the Princess might see the Queen her mother, – which he at first refused, and on my making some remonstrance he said he would take advice on the subject. The Princess had advised me to make this request. London, 30 Dec. 1535.[6]

It is heartbreaking to read of the man who had once loved her and who Catherine still loved regarding her as nothing more than an obstacle in his life. The golden prince of their early days together had almost certainly vanished and we must ask ourselves if they had ever come face to face what Catherine would have thought – would she have recognised him?

Upon receiving permission, Chapuys immediately set off for Kimbolton. But someone else, apart from Chapuys and Mary, was eager to see Catherine one last time. In a letter also dated 30 December, a Lady Mary Wyllughby (Willoughby) wrote to Cromwell:

> *When I sent my servant to you he brought me word that you were in such importunate business that you could not despatch me or any other body. But now I must put you to pain, for I heard that my mistress is very sore sick again. I pray you remember me, for you promised to labor with the king to get me licence to go to her before God send for her, as there is no other likliehood. Unless the King will let me have a letter to show the officers of my mistresses house my licence will be of no effect. No one can help me so well as yourself. Barbican 30, Dec.*[7]

Lady Mary Willoughby was the former Maria de Salinas who had come to England either with Catherine, or shortly after, to serve her. The two had been forced to part in 1532 when Henry had reduced Catherine's household and Maria had not seen her mistress since; now she was determined to do so.

Chapuys arrived at Kimbolton on 2 January and had his first audience with her after dinner. They were closely observed by her steward, Sir Henry Bedingfield, and her chamberlain who had not seen her for more than a year despite living in the same property. This was a sure sign of how reclusive Catherine had become, as of course Bedingfield was Henry's man[8] and did not recognise her as queen. Whilst they likely did not have much choice in this observance, Catherine told Chapuys she wanted witnesses so that her husband would know they did not plot against him and that she was not exaggerating her illness. On their reunion they did not discuss contentious matters, merely

Queen Catherine of Aragon by John Cassell, c.1865. From Cassell's *Illustrated History of England*, Volume 2. (*Public Domain image, via Wikimedia Commons*)

greeting each other and Catherine thanked Chapuys for all the trouble he had taken on her behalf, she continued:

> … *if it pleased God to take her, it would be a consolation to her to die under my guidance (entre mes braz) and not unprepared, like a beast.*

Chapuys reassured her on her health and begged her to get well for 'the union and peace of Christendom depended on her life'. He also claimed, kindly but untruthfully, that Henry was very sorry to hear of her illness and that they had discussed moving her to another better property and that he would pay the arrears in her funds. It was a short meeting and Catherine bid Chapuys to rest following his journey; meanwhile she would sleep a little herself as she told him she had not slept well the last few days.[9]

Catherine would not be abandoned like a beast, as Maria de Salinas had arrived the day before him. She had not waited for permission and had set out for Kimbolton on her own initiative. Perhaps her instinct told her time was running out, and we don't know if she would have been granted permission to visit Catherine even if she had waited. In what was perhaps the greatest unpunished trick ever pulled on Henry, Maria had arrived looking quite downtrodden and covered in mud. She claimed that she had fallen from her horse and that the passport she had been issued from the king had been lost in the fall but her servants were looking for it and would bring it along shortly. Seeing this respected woman looking less than her best, Bedingfield admitted her to the house, Maria took her chance and promptly disappeared into Catherine's chamber and did not come out again.[10]

Perhaps Maria did fall from her horse, but it's equally possible that she 'roughed' herself up to gain sympathy and admittance to Kimbolton. What is certainly true is that she did not ever have permission or a licence to visit Catherine, but loyalty to her mistress won out and Maria was determined she was going to be there for her. This was a touching display of loyalty that resonates today and one for which Henry never punished her for.

Chapuys stayed with Catherine for four days, finally departing on 5 January, and during that time, according to his own report, he had multiple discussions with her. Catherine had started to worry that perhaps she was to blame for the state of the kingdom and the heresies that were now flourishing in it, but Chapuys was able to reassure her:

> *I spent full two hours in conversation with her, and though I several times wished to leave her for fear of wearying her, I could not do so, she said it was*

so great a pleasure and consolation. I spent the same period of time with her every day of the four days I staid there. She inquired about the health of your Majesty and the state of your affairs, and regretted her misfortune and that of the Princess, and the delay of remedy by which all good men had suffered in person and in goods, and so many ladies were going to perdition. But, on my showing her that your Majesty could not have done better than you had done hitherto, considering the great affairs which had hindered you, and also that the delay had not been without advantages (for, besides there being some hope that the French, who formerly solicited the favour of this King, would now turn their backs, there was this, that the Pope, by reason of the death of the cardinal of Rochester, and other disorders, intended to seek a remedy in the name of the Holy See, and thus, preparations being made at the instance of the Holy See, the King could not blame her as the cause), she was quite satisfied and thought the delay had been for the best. And as to the heresies here [I said] she knew well that God said there must of necessity be heresies and slanders for the exaltation of the good and confusion of the wicked, and that she must consider that the heresies were not so rooted here that they would not soon be remedied, and that it was to be hoped that those who had been deluded would afterwards be the most firm, like St. Peter after he had tripped. Of these words she showed herself very glad, for she had previously had some scruple of conscience because [the heresies] had arisen from her affair.[11]

Chapuys departed on 5 January as Catherine seemed better. She was now eating and sleeping more and was increasingly cheerful, and Chapuys did not want to be accused of abusing the licence Henry had given him as he never knew when he may need Henry's permission to visit her again. He asked her physician to keep him informed of any changes before departing, leaving Catherine to the care of Maria and her few loyal attendants.

The next day, Catherine was able to sit up and comb and dress her own hair but by nighttime something had changed, and Catherine seemed to know her end was near. After midnight she repeatedly asked for the time as she wished to hear Mass and receive the Sacrament, but this could not be performed before dawn. Her confessor, Jorge de Athequa, Bishop of Llandaff, clearly as anxious as Catherine, offered to celebrate it at 4 a.m. but she would not hear of it, quoting scripture as to why he could not do so. When dawn finally came, she heard Mass and took the Sacrament 'with the utmost fervour, and thereafter continued to repeat some beautiful orisons, and begged the bystanders to pray for her soul'. She told those around her 'that God would pardon the King her husband the wrong he had done her, and that the divine goodness would lead him to the true road and give him good counsel'.[12]

Before he had departed Kimbolton, Chapuys had asked Catherine's confessor that if she sickened again and it looked as if she was not going to recover, he was to extract from her an oath that she had never consummated her marriage to Prince Arthur. A deathbed oath or confession carried a lot of weight in Tudor times as it was believed the dying person would not jeopardise their soul just before they were about to meet their maker. Sadly, whether through distraction at what was taking place or concern for upsetting Catherine in her final moments, her confessor did not perform this request.[13]

Catherine was able to set down a few requests regarding her servants and the distribution of the belongings she still possessed. She could not write a will as she still regarded herself as a married woman, but she could leave a list of bequests. Shortly after this, it is believed Catherine wrote or dictated one final letter to the man she still loved. Whilst there are doubts as to its authenticity, historians generally agree the sentiments written within it are recognisable as Catherine's:

Catherine of Aragon by Robert White, after Hans Holbein the Younger, year unknown. The image incorrectly records Catherine's death as 8 January. (*Source Wellcome Collection — CC 4.0 Public Domain image, via Wikimedia Commons*)

My most dear lord, king and husband,
The hour of my death now drawing on, the tender love I owe you forceth me, my case being such, to commend myself to you, and to put you in remembrance with a few words of the health and safeguard of your soul which you ought to prefer before all worldly matters, and before the care and pampering of your body, for the which you have cast me into many calamities and yourself into many troubles. For my part, I pardon you everything, and I wish to devoutly pray God that He will pardon you also. For the rest, I commend unto you our daughter Mary, beseeching you to be a good father unto her, as I have heretofore desired. I entreat you also, on behalf of my maids, to give them marriage portions, which is not much, they being but three. For all my other servants I solicit the

wages due them, and a year more, lest they be unprovided for. Lastly, I make this vow, that mine eyes desire you above all things.
   Katharine the Quene.[14]

Catherine of Aragon peacefully slipped away at around 2 p.m. on 7 January 1536; she was 50 years old. To the end, she maintained that she was Henry's true wife and queen and her daughter, Mary, Henry and England's heir.

Chapter 10

Afterlife

The news of Catherine's death reached Henry the next day, but it was left to Cromwell to break the sad news to Chapuys who informed the Emperor:

He [Cromwell] sent to inform me of the lamentable news of the death of the most virtuous Queen, which took place on Friday the morrow of the Kings, about 2 p.m. This has been the most cruel news that could come to me, especially as I fear the good Princess will die of grief, or that the concubine will hasten what she has long threatened to do, viz., to kill her; and it is to be feared that there is little help for it. I will do my best to comfort her, in which a letter from your Majesty would help greatly. I cannot relate in detail the circumstances of the Queen's decease, nor how she has disposed of her affairs, for none of her servants has yet come. I know not if they have been detained.

He later wrote:

The Queen's illness began about five weeks ago, as I then wrote to your Majesty, and the attack was renewed on the morrow of Christmas day. It was a pain in the stomach, so violent that she could retain no food. I asked her physician several times if there was any suspicion of poison. He said he was afraid it was so, for after she had drunk some Welsh beer she had been worse, and that it must have been a slow and subtle poison for he could not discover evidences of simple and pure poison; but on opening her, indications will be seen.[1]

As noted earlier, rumours of plots and assassinations almost always circulated when a high personage became an obstacle or died at too convenient a time for their enemies and seemingly proof of poison was found when Catherine's body was opened in preparation for her funeral. The grim duty of embalming was performed by the wax chandler and plumber; Catherine's confessor and her doctors were not allowed to be present.[2] This was taken to mean that there was something to hide, but was likely done to prevent the spreading of rumours, in which case they failed. The speed of her embalming was also commented on but this can be explained away as usual procedure as dictated by the Royal Book.

Upon first examination, it looked as if all Catherine's internal organs were completely normal until they came to her heart 'which was quite black and hideous to look at'. The Chandler washed it multiple times, but its colour did not change and upon slicing it open he discovered it was the same colour throughout. A 'black round thing which clung closely to the outside' was also noted. This was taken as evidence of poison, but modern medical opinion commonly agrees that Catherine likely died from a form of cancer. It can be claimed that Catherine of Aragon died of a broken heart. After the examination was complete, Catherine's body was 'sered, tramayled, leded, and chested with spices'; she was then carried to the chapel at Kimbolton where her body was placed beneath a hearse surrounded by torches and watched over by her remaining loyal servants.[3]

Catherine of Aragon by the Printmaker, Cornelis Martinus Vermeulen, after a painting by Adriaen van der Werff, c.1697. (*Public Domain image, via Wikimedia Commons*)

Henry and Anne did not help the rumours by distastefully celebrating Catherine's death. Anne rewarded the messenger who brought her the news and reports survive that state either Henry or Anne, or both, dressed in yellow in celebration. Henry was heard to say 'God be praised that we are free from all suspicion of war' and looked forward to being able to renew his previously good relationship with Catherine's nephew. Anne's father and brother commented that 'it was a pity that the Princess [Mary] did not keep company with her'. The Sunday after Catherine's death saw Henry showing off his younger daughter to the court and dancing with the ladies present.[4]

However, Anne quickly became subdued and its likely she realised that Catherine's death, rather than securing her own queenship and marriage, had left her dangerously exposed. Henry and Anne's marriage was not as happy as it once had been, and whilst Catherine lived Henry would have found it very difficult, if not impossible, to set aside her aside and marry a third wife; it would have made him the laughing stock of England and of Europe, something Henry could never abide. If he had ended his marriage to Anne he would have faced unbearable pressure to return to Catherine, another course of action equally unattractive to him as he would essentially have had to admit he was wrong to marry Anne and set aside Catherine. With Catherine's death, Henry did not have the latter issue to contend with and as most of England and Europe did not recognise his second marriage, and in fact regarded Henry as a widower upon Catherine's death, the former was also now less of an issue as well. Henry's second marriage could easily be swept aside and, in time-honoured tradition, perhaps blamed on the advice of bad councillors. There would have been some adverse comments, but nothing to the scale he would have had to have faced

Peterborough Cathedral. Peterborough Abbey, as it was then known, was chosen by Henry for Catherine's final resting place. (*Attribution David Iliff, Wikimedia, CC 3.0; Public Domain image, via Wikimedia Commons*)

if he had two ex-wives living. Anne did still have a trump card; she was once again pregnant. Now her queenship and her marriage rested on ensuring this pregnancy was successful and produced the much needed and wanted male heir.

In a macabre twist, it would seem Catherine had her revenge from beyond the grave.

Catherine's funeral took place on 29 January. She had requested that she be laid to rest in a convent of Observant Friars, but unbeknownst to her these had all recently been suppressed. Instead she was laid to rest where her funeral was held, in Peterborough Abbey, now Peterborough Cathedral. She had asked that 500 masses be said for her soul and that 'some personage go to our Lady of Walsingham on pilgrimage and distribute 20 nobles on the way', though whether this was undertaken is not known.[5]

No expenses were spared for Catherine's funeral – three chariots were provided, one to carry her to her final resting place, the others for the noblemen and mourners. Four knights were required to 'bear a canopy over it [Catherines body], six knights to bear the body and six barons to assist'. Torches were provided for the yeoman escorting the cortege and lit in the towns she would pass through on her last journey, whilst nine were provided in the Abbey where she was to be buried. Banners including her personal symbol of the pomegranate and the coats of arms of England and Spain were carried in the procession and later displayed at the abbey. Her chief mourner was to ride on a horse draped in black cloth and accompanied by eight ladies riding close behind her equally dressed in black. Black cloth was also provided for thirty ladies and gentlemen mourners, the noblemen present and her officers and 'liveries for dukes or duchesses, earls, &c., cloth for themselves and for a number of servants according to their degrees'.

Another hearse was required to receive her body at the abbey, with double barriers built around it for the ladies and lords that were attending her funeral. Catherine did not have an effigy but a 'puffed image of a Princess' and a pall 'four gentlemen to bear at the four corners'. Arrangements were made for Catherine to be watched over during the night prior to her funeral.[6]

It was a grand funeral but it was not one befitting a queen but a princess dowager. Henry was using Catherine's funeral to reinforce her status as decreed by him to the world and for that reason Chapuys did not attend, he decided instead to mourn in private. Maria de Salinas did choose to attend, alongside her daughter, the new Duchess of Suffolk, who saw her own stepdaughter, Henry's niece Eleanor Brandon, act as Catherine's chief mourner. The sermon was preached by John Hilsey, Bishop of Rochester who disgraced himself by saying that at the end Catherine had acknowledged that she had never been queen of England,[7] a blatant lie that no one in the congregation believed. To Henry's credit, he wore black the day of Catherine's internment and attended a Mass in her honour, but Anne reportedly wore yellow again and complained that all anyone spoke about was the good end her rival had made.

Mary was not allowed to attend her mother's funeral.

On the same day that Catherine was laid to rest, Anne Boleyn suffered a miscarriage. She claimed it was caused by the fright she had had upon learning Henry had suffered a fall whilst he was jousting. Unfortunately for Anne, two sources indicate that the baby she lost was a boy. Chapuys wrote on 10 February to the Emperor that:

On the day of the interment [Catherine's funeral] the Concubine had an abortion which seemed to be a male child which she had not borne 3½ months, at which the King has shown great distress. The said concubine wished to lay the blame on the duke of Norfolk, whom she hates, saying he frightened her by bringing the news of the fall the King had six days before. But it is well known that is not the cause, for it was told her in a way that she should not be alarmed or attach much importance to it. Some think it was owing to her own incapacity to bear children, others to a fear that the King would treat her like the late Queen, especially considering the treatment shown to a lady of the Court, named Mistress Semel [Jane Seymour], to whom, as many say, he has lately made great presents.[8]

The Tudor Chronicler, Charles Wriothesley, also documented the same tragic event writing:

This yeare also, three daies before Candlemas, Queene Anne was brought a bedd and delivered of a man chield, as it was said, afore her tyme, for she said that she had reckoned herself at that tyme but fiftene weekes gonne with child; it was said she tooke a fright, for the King ranne that tjrme at the ring and had a fall from his horse, but he had no hurt; and she tooke such a fright withall that it caused her to fall in travaile, and so was delivered afore her full tyme, which was a great discompfort to all this realme.

Anne would never have another child; just four months after Catherine's death, she was executed at the Tower of London on what are widely believed to be trumped up charges of adultery, incest and treason. Strangely, there is an account of a French man writing to Thomas Cromwell that the day before Anne's execution 'the wax tapers about Q. Catherine's tomb had been lighted of their own accord'.[9] Eleven days later, Henry married his third wife, Jane Seymour. Jane had served in the households of both Catherine and Anne but was known to be a supporter of the former and her daughter. She interceded for Mary with her father, but Henry demanded Mary's complete and utter surrender to his will; he would only take her back into his fatherly affections if she recognised him as Supreme Head of the Church in England and admitted that her mother's marriage was invalid and she was therefore illegitimate. To Henry's fury, Mary refused once again and for a short, tense time it looked as if Henry would proceed against his daughter to the full extent of the law.[10]

Mary was in a heartbreaking position. She loved both of her parents but firmly sided with her mother and believed her father had been wrong to set Catherine aside. She trusted that their marriage had been good and valid from the start, and she believed herself to be legitimate and the true heir to the throne of England. Her mother had constantly bid her to 'answer with few words' and obey her father in everything, except when the action could offend God and jeopardise her soul. She was to 'go no further with learning and disputation in the matter. And wheresoever, and in whatsoever company you shall come. Speak you few words and meddle nothing'.[11]

Mary had Catherine's example before her; she had not given up her beliefs or rights and had maintained them until the day she died, but in the months since her mother's death Mary's situation had become very different. She was grief-stricken and alone, and she did not have her mother's love and support to fall back on; her friends and allies were also under attack. She was also faced with the fact that her father had just had the women he once loved executed – who was to say he would not proceed against his daughter in the same way?

With a heavy heart, Mary gave up her and her mother's fight, signing the articles presented to her. By signing, she fully recognised Henry as her sovereign and all his laws; she acknowledged him to be the Supreme Head of the Church of England under Christ, and repudiated the 'pretended authority of the bishop of Rome'. Most upsetting of all, she agreed that the marriage between the king and her beloved mother had never been valid and was in fact 'by God's law and man's law incestuous and unlawful'.

Mary would never forgive herself and was observed to be sorrowful for a time after. Chapuys attempted to console her by telling her the Pope would understand and even provide a dispensation for her actions, as they were taken under duress. Shortly after, Mary was welcomed back at court and reunited with her father. She was recognised as the first lady of the land after Queen Jane, and the two struck up a close and loving friendship. Mary was devastated when Jane died just over a year later, after giving Henry his longed-for heart's desire, Mary's half-brother, Prince Edward.

Mary watched Henry marry three more times in an attempt to have another son, but he would prove unsuccessful. He died on 28 January 1547, eleven years after Catherine, and was succeed by Jane's son, Edward, who became King Edward VI. Mary had doted on Edward when he was young, but as his reign

Queen Mary I, Antonis Mor, c.1554. Mary did finally become queen in 1553, fulfilling her mother's hopes and dreams, but her reign would be short and overshadowed by her more famous half-sister. (*Public Domain image, via Wikimedia Commons*)

progressed the pressures of kingship and the Reformation tore their relationship apart, as Edward became more vocal in his Protestant beliefs and moved the Church of England in that direction. Tragically Edward died in July 1553, aged just 15, but before he died, he attempted to change the succession and leave the throne to a protestant heir: their cousin the Lady Jane Grey.

Though he never legitimised them, Mary and Elizabeth had been reinstated to the line of succession by their father in 1543, and Edward knew that if Mary inherited his throne all his work would be undone, and she would bring England back to Rome. Edward's plan failed and Lady Jane Grey was deposed in a bloodless coup after the people rallied behind Mary, recognising her as England's first queen regnant.

Mary had come to the throne, as her mother had always wanted, and she had not forgotten her duty to her. Her first parliament in October 1553 repealed the legislation declaring Henry and Catherine's marriage void, thereby pronouncing it valid. Catherine was restored to her rightful place as Henry's wife and queen of England and Mary their lawful heir.

Mary would reign over England for just five years and has been written off as a failure, but her reign is currently undergoing a reassessment. It is true that England's last outpost on the Continent, Calais, was lost on her watch and her attempts to reimpose Catholicism led to the horrific burning of possibly 300 men and women, earning her the nickname Bloody Mary. But it seems strange that neither her father nor her sister have earned the nicknames 'Bloody Henry' or 'Bloody Elizabeth' when they oversaw the executions of significantly more people during their respective reigns. Time was Mary's enemy, as her attempts to reinstate Catholicism may have been successful if she had lived longer; Protestantism was not as widespread across England as first thought and her attempts were generally greeted with acceptance, but later propaganda would ensure Mary was condemned for her actions.

During her reign Mary was able to restructure the economy, reorganise the militia and rebuild the Navy, but perhaps most importantly of all, she restored the Tudor succession as her father had intended and in doing so ensured that her own sister would inherit in time. She set the precedents Elizabeth would later rely on, though never acknowledge or appear grateful for.[12]

Before her death, she asked that Catherine's body be moved from Peterborough to Westminster Abbey to rest alongside her own, reuniting them both in death as they couldn't be in life; it was a wish that was never granted.[13]

In 1587, the now known Peterborough Cathedral saw the internment of another discarded queen: Mary Queen of Scots. Mary had been executed 6 months earlier at Fotheringhay Castle for her attempts to usurp the throne of Mary's half-sister and successor, Elizabeth I. Her body had lain unburied until a decision was made on where to lay her remains to rest; eventually Peterborough Cathedral was chosen.[14] Mary's resting place was directly opposite Catherine and by strange coincidence the same man who interred her had also interred Catherine fifty-one years earlier.

The site of Mary, Queen of Scots' former resting place. (*Reproduced with kind permission from Peterborough Cathedral*)

Robert Scarlett, known locally as Old Scarlett, is the man who holds this dubious honour, but he always claimed that he had interred three queens, as he had also interred his first wife there too. Scarlett lived until he was 98, truly impressive for Tudor times, and managed to witness the reigns of all five Tudor monarchs. He was born in 1496 and died in 1594. For his loyalty and dedication to Peterborough, he was himself interred in the cathedral where a fresco celebrating his life can still be seen.[15]

For twenty-five years Catherine and Mary lay together at Peterborough, until Mary's son King James VI and I of Scotland and England, disinterred his mother and had her reburied in Westminster Abbey, close to Elizabeth I. Catherine's grave was not disturbed at this time.

Nine years into his reign, Henry began plans for a grand tomb for himself and Catherine, believing they would rest together for eternity as the mother and father of the next king of England. The tomb was to be designed by Pietro Torrigiano, the same man who had designed his parents' tomb, but it was to be 25 per cent bigger. If you are lucky enough to visit Westminster Abbey today, you can get an idea of the size Henry had in mind. Following a financial disagreement, Torrigiano left the project and England, and the next documented report we have of the tomb is from 1527 when another Italian Sculptor, Jacopo Sansovino, was considering taking it on.[16] Soon after, events would overtake the project and by Catherine's death in 1536, something quite different was needed. It seems a monument was erected to Catherine's memory, but it is long gone, destroyed by Oliver Cromwell's troops during the English Civil War. The Reverend W. D. Sweeting wrote about Catherine's burial and monument in his book *The Cathedral Church of Peterborough: A description of its fabric and a brief history of the Episcopal See*:

> *Queen Katherine of Arragon [sic] was buried in the north choir aisle, just outside the most eastern arch, in 1535. A hearse was placed near, probably between the two piers. Four years later this is described as 'the inclosed place where the Lady Katherine lieth,' and there seems to have been a small altar within it. Some banners that adorned it remained in the cathedral till 1586. About the same time some persons were imprisoned for defacing the 'monument,' and required to 'reform the same.' The only monument, strictly so called, of which there is any record, was a low table monument, raised on two shallow steps, with simple quatrefoils, carved in squares set diamond-wise. Engravings of this shew it to have been an insignificant and mean erection. A few slabs of it were lately found buried beneath the floor, and they are now placed against the wall of the aisle. One of the prebendaries repaired this monument at his own cost, about 1725, and supplied a tiny brass plate with name and date, part of which remains in the floor. This monument was removed in 1792. A handsome marble stone has*

Tomb of Queen Catherine of Aragon at Peterborough Cathedral. (*David Iliff, Wikimedia, CC BY-SA 3.0; Public Domain image, via Wikimedia Commons*)

quite recently been laid down to the Queen's memory above her grave, with incised inscription and coats of arms.[17]

As we can see, Catherines monument has been vandalised and restored a few times but her tomb was opened for the first and last time in 1777 to satisfy an urban legend: it was believed that Catherine's loyal lady-in-waiting, Maria de Salinas, had been laid to rest alongside her after she died in 1539. When the tomb was opened, however, only one coffin was found: Catherine's. It was thought disrespectful to actually open her coffin but supposedly a small hole was drilled into the side of it and then a small hook inserted which pulled out a portion of Catherine's robe. The robe was described as black and silver brocade but quickly disintegrated upon being exposed to the air. Catherine's coffin was quickly resealed and so was her tomb and she has not been disturbed since. In this, she is more fortunate than some of Henry's other wives.[18]

Wax model of Catherine of Aragon. Catherine can be found in several exhibits as a waxwork, not just in England but worldwide. (*Source George S. Stuart Historical Figures; photographed by Peter d'Aprix and Dee Finning. Owned by Museum of Ventura County. Wikimedia, CC 3.0. Public Domain image, via Wikimedia Commons*)

The monument we see today was installed in the nineteenth century. Its creation was brought about by the wife of one of the cathedral canons, Katharine Clayton, who launched a public appeal asking women with the name Catherine, or variations of it, to donate towards a memorial to the former much-loved queen. The marble slab and gilded letters we see today are the result of Katharine Clayton's campaign.[19]

A memorial plaque nearby reads:

A queen cherished by the English people for her loyalty, piety, courage and compassion.

Catherine is still a part of our lives today. Every year on the weekend nearest 29 January, the anniversary of her burial, Peterborough Cathedral holds the 'Katharine of Aragon Festival'. The festival consists of talks, tours and activities for children but also a commemoration service and a Roman Catholic Mass that is attended by the Spanish ambassador or a representative of the Spanish embassy. It is rare to see her tomb without flowers or pomegranates.[20]

It will be noticed by anyone who has been fortunate enough to visit the cathedral, or even seen pictures, that above her grave is her name and the title she believed was rightfully hers: Katharine, Queen of England. There are also banners depicting the arms of England and Spain. Another queen consort, Mary of Teck, queen of George V, ordered that the symbols of queenship and the banners be hung above her tomb depicting to the world Catherine's status as queen of England and a Spanish Infanta.[21, 22]

In death, Catherine has been restored to her rightful place.

A portrait formerly believed to be of King Henry VIII's last wife, Queen Katherine Parr, but re-identified as Queen Catherine of Aragon in 2012. Portrait by an unknown artist (British 'English' School?) c.1520. This portrait is Catherine as she would wish to be remembered … as the queen. (*Public Domain image, via Wikimedia Commons*)

Appendices

Appendix 1

A Comprehensive List of Preparations for Catherine's Funeral

'Provision to be made for bowelling, coring, and enclosing the corpse in lead. For lights and other things about the corpse, in the house, or the next church or chapel, and who shall execute exequies and ceremonies. Proportions for all manner of lights, and for blacks to be distributed. What personages, and how many personages, women, to be appointed as principal mourners. How many chariots shall follow the corpse, and what apparel shall be appointed for them. Where the body shall be interred. How many prelates shall be present at the interment. What dole shall be dealt in every place, and in pence, half groats, or groats, or in all after the diversity of the place.'

Letters to be made for the appointment of such personages of honour as shall be at the same.

Written in Wriothesley's hand.

'A remembrance for thenterrement of the right excellent and noble Princesse the Lady Catherin, Doughter to the right highe and mighty Prince Ferdinand, late King of Castle, and late Wief to the noble and excellent prince Arthur, Brother to our Soveraign Lorde King Henry the viijth.'

Directions as to the corpse being 'sered, tramayled, leded, and chested with spices, &c.;' for a hearse 'with five principalles and lights' to be set in the church or chapel where the body shall first remain, and another 'with nine principalls or lights' in the church where it shall be buried; for staff torches to be borne by yeomen and long torches in great towns as the body shall pass; for wax; for double barriers about the principal hearse, the inner for ladies and the outer for lords.

At the removal the body is to be attended by three mutes; divers noblemen and four knights to bear a canopy over it, six knights to bear the body and six barons to assist. The chief mourner and eight others to accompany the corpse. Arrangements for nightly watch, chariot to convey the corpse, with pall and puffed image of a Princess; four gentlemen to bear at the four corners, &c. 'The chief mourner on horseback, her horse trapped with black velvet to follow immediately the corpse,' with eight ladies after her on palfreys trapped in black cloth. Two other chariots to follow.

- ii. 'The painter's charge;' for the supply of banners and scutcheons.
- iii. 'The charges of the wardrobe.' To provide cloth for 30 ladies and gentlemen mourners, and for the noblemen present, and for her officers.
- iv. 'The rate of the liveries' for dukes or duchesses, earls, &c., cloth for themselves and for a number of servants according to their degrees.
- v. 'To be also remembered.' To appoint prelates to execute for the time she shall be unburied, &c.; also touching doles and various other matters; among others what place the body shall be interred in.

'The 25th day of this present month of January, it is commanded that all such stuff as is committed to the doings of the chandler, the painter, the saddler, and all other having anything to be done touching the interment, shall be ready and bestowed in such places as be to them appointed for the same.'

In Wriothesley's hand.

Source: Letters and Papers, Foreign and Domestic, Henry VIII, Volume 10, January–June 1536. Documents 38 and 39 – [Katharine of Arragon?] and Burial of Katharine of Arragon, dated January 1536.

Appendix 2

Will of Katharine of Arragon

Desires the King to let her have the goods she holds of him in gold and silver and the money due to her in time past; that her body may be buried in a convent of Observant Friars; that 500 masses be said for her soul; that some personage go to our Lady of Walsingham on pilgrimage and distribute 20 nobles on the way. Bequests: to Mrs. Darel 200*l*. for her marriage. To my daughter, the collar of gold which I brought out of Spain. To Mrs. Blanche 100*l*. To Mrs. Margery and Mrs. [Whyller] 40*l*. each. To Mrs. Mary, my physicians [wife, and] Mrs. Isabel, daughter to Mr. Ma[rguerite], 40*l*. each. To ray physician the year's coming [wages]. To Francisco Philippo all that I owe him, and 40*l*. besides. To Master John, my apothecary, [a year's wages] and all that is due to him besides. That Mr. Whiller be paid expenses about the making of my gown, and 20*l*. besides. To Philip, Anthony, and Bastian, 20*l*. each. To the little maidens 10*l*. each. That my goldsmith be paid his wages for the year coming and all that is due to him besides. That my lavander be paid what is due to her and her wages for the year coming. To Isabel of Vergas 20*l*. To my ghostly father his wages for the year coming. That ornaments be made of my gowns for the convent where I shall be [buried] 'and the furs of the same 1 give to my daughter.' [Note: page 2 of the document is mutilated.]

Source: Letters and Papers, Foreign and Domestic, Henry VIII, Volume 10, January–June 1536. Document 40 – Will of Katharine of Arragon.

Appendix 3

Detailed Report of Catherine of Aragon's Funeral

The good Queen died in a few days, of God knows what illness, on Friday, 7 Jan. 1536. Next day her body was taken into the Privy Chamber and placed under the canopy of State (*sous le dhoussier et drapt destat*), where it rested seven days, without any other solemnity than four flambeaux continually burning. During this time a leaden coffin was prepared, in which the body was enclosed on Saturday, the 15th, and borne to the chapel. The vigils of the dead were said the same day, and next day one mass and no more, without any other light than six torches of rosin.

On Sunday, the 16th, the body was removed again into the Privy Chamber, where it remained till Saturday following. Meanwhile an 'estalage,' which we call a *chapelle ardente*, was arranged, with 56 wax candles in all, and the house hung with two breadths of the lesser frieze of the country. On Saturday, the 22nd, it was again brought to the chapel, and remained until the masses of Thursday following, during which time solemn masses were said in the manner of the country, at which there assisted by turns as principals the duchess of Suffolk, the countess of Worcester, the young countess of Oxford, the countess of Surrey, and baronesses Howard, Willoughby, Bray, and Gascon (*sic*).

On Tuesday following as they were beginning mass, four banners of crimson taffeta were brought, two of which bore the arms of the Queen, one those of England, with three 'lambeaulx blancs,' which they say are of prince Arthur; the fourth had the two, viz., of Spain and England, together. There were also four great golden [standards]. On one was painted the Trinity, on the second Our Lady, on the third St. Katharine, and on the fourth St. George; and by the side of these representations the said arms were depicted in the above order; and in like manner the said arms were simply, and without gilding (? *dourance*), painted and set over all the house, and above them a simple crown, distinguished from that of the kingdom which is closed.

On Wednesday after the robes of the Queen's 10 ladies were completed, who had not till then made any mourning, except with kerchiefs on their heads and old robes. This day, at dinner, the countess of Surrey held state, who at the vigils after dinner was chief mourner. On Thursday, after mass, which was no less solemn than the vigils of the day before, the body was carried from the chapel and put on a waggon, to be conveyed not to one of the convents of the Observant Friars, as the Queen had desired before her death, but at the pleasure of the King, her husband, to the Benedictine Abbey of Peterborough, and they departed in the following order: – First, 16 priests or clergymen in surplices went on horseback, without saying a word, having a gilded laten cross borne before them; after them several gentlemen, of whom there were only two of the house, 'et le demeurant estoient tous emprouvez,' and after them followed the maître d'hotel and chamberlain, with their rods of office in their hands; and, to keep them in order, went by their sides 9 or 10 heralds, with mourning hoods and wearing their coats of arms; after them followed 50 servants of the aforesaid gentlemen, bearing torches and 'bâtons allumés,' which lasted but a short time, and in the middle of them was drawn a waggon, upon which the body was drawn by six horses all covered with black cloth to the ground.

The said waggon was covered with black velvet, in the midst of which was a great silver cross; and within, as one looked upon the corpse, was stretched a cloth of gold frieze with a cross of crimson velvet, and before and behind the said waggon stood two gentlemen ushers with mourning hoods looking into the waggon, round which the said four banners were carried by four heralds and the standards with the representations by four gentlemen. Then followed seven ladies, as chief mourners, upon hackneys, that of the first being harnessed with black velvet and the others with black cloth. After which ladies followed the waggon of the Queen's gentlemen; and after them, on hackneys, came nine ladies, wives of knights. Then followed the waggon of the Queen's chambermaids; then her maids to the number of 36, and in their wake followed certain servants on horseback.

In this order the royal corpse was conducted for nine miles of the country, *i.e.*, three French leagues, as far as the abbey of Sautry, where the abbot and his monks received it and placed it under a canopy in the choir of the church, under an 'estalage' prepared for it, which contained 408 candles, which burned during the vigils that day and next day at mass. Next day a solemn mass was chanted in the said abbey of Sautry, by the bishop of Ely, during which in the middle of the church 48 torches of rosin were carried by as many poor men, with mourning hoods and garments.

After mass the body was borne in the same order to the abbey of Peterborough, where at the door of the church it was honorably received by the bishops of Lincoln, Ely, and Rochester, the abbot of the place, and the abbots of Ramsey, Crolain (Crowland), Tournan (Thorney), Walden and Thaem (Tame), who, wearing their mitres and hoods, accompanied it in procession till it was placed under the *chapelle ardente* which was prepared for it there, upon eight pillars of beautiful fashion and roundness, upon which were placed about 1,000 candles, both little and middle-sized, and round about the said chapel 18 banners waved, of which one bore the arms of the Emperor, a second those of England, with those of the King's mother, prince Arthur, the queen of Portugal, sister of the deceased, Spain, Arragon, and Sicily, and those of Spain and England with three 'lambeaulx,' those of John of Gaunt, duke of Lancaster, who married the daughter of Peter the Cruel, viz., 'le joux des beufz,' the bundle of arrows, the pomegranate (*granade*), the lion and the greyhound. Likewise there were a great number of little pennons, in which were portrayed the devices of king Ferdinand, father of the deceased, and of herself; and round about the said chapel, in great gold letters was written, as the device of the said good lady, 'Humble et loyale.'

Solemn vigils were said that day, and on the morrow the three masses by three bishops: the first by the bishop of Rochester, with the abbot of Thame as deacon, and the abbot of Walden as sub-deacon; the second by the bishop of Ely, with the abbot of Tournay (Thorney) as deacon, and the abbot of Peterborough as sub-deacon; the third by the bishop of Lincoln, with the bishop of Llandaff as deacon, and that of Ely as sub-deacon; the other bishops and abbots aforesaid assisting at the said masses in their pontificals, so the ceremony was very sumptuous. The chief mourner was lady Eleanor, daughter of the duke of Suffolk and the French queen, and niece of king Henry, widower now of the said good Queen. She was conducted to the offering by the Comptroller and Mr. Gust (Gostwick), new receiver of the moneys the King takes from the Church. Immediately after the offering was completed the bishop of Rochester preached the same as all the preachers of England for two years have not ceased to preach, viz., against the power of the Pope, whom they call bishop of Rome, and against the marriage of the said good Queen and the King, alleging against all truth that in the hour of death she acknowledged she had not been queen of England. I say against all truth, because at that hour she ordered a writing to be made in her name addressed to the King as her husband, and to the ambassador of the Emperor, her nephew, which she signed with these words – Katharine, queen of England – commending her ladies and servants to the favor of the said ambassador.

At the end of the mass all the mourning ladies offered in the hands of the heralds each three ells in three pieces of cloth of gold which were upon the body, and of this '*accoutrements*' will be made for the chapel where the annual service will be performed for her. After the mass the body was buried in a grave at the lowest step of the high altar, over which they put a simple black cloth. In this manner was celebrated the funeral of her who for 27 years has been true queen of England, whose holy soul, as every one must believe, is in eternal rest, after worldly misery borne by her with such patience that there is little need to pray God for her; to whom, nevertheless, we ought incessantly to address prayers for the weal (*salut*) of her living image whom she has left to us, the most virtuous Princess her daughter, that He may comfort her in her great and infinite adversities, and give her a husband to his pleasure, &c.

Fr., from a modern copy, p.6.

Source: Letters and Papers, Foreign and Domestic, Henry VIII, Volume 10, January–June 1536. Documents 284 – Death and Burial of Katharine of Arragon, dated 10 February 1536 (Vienna Archives).

Appendix 4

Excerpt from a Letter Written by Jean De Ponte to Thomas Cromwell Regarding the Tapers at Catherines Tomb

'During dinner a servant of the master of the Maison Dieu, named Tra[sse], came in with news that the day before Madame Anne was beheaded, the tapers at the sepulchre of queen Katharine lighted of themselves, and, after matins, at *Deo Gratias*, went out; that the King sent 30 men to the abbey where queen Katharine was buried to inquire about it, and the light continued from day to day; that orders would soon be issued to pray for queen Katharine as before.'

Source: Letters and Papers, Foreign and Domestic, Henry VIII, Volume 10, January–June 1536. Documents 1023 – Jean De Ponte to Cromwell, dated 1 June 1536

Appendix 5

Excerpt from the Last Will and Testament of Queen Mary I Regarding her Desire to be Laid to Rest Alongside her Mother

'And further I will that the body of the vertuous Lady and my most dere and well-beloved mother of happy memory, Quene Kateryn, whych lyeth now buried at Peterborowh, shall within as short tyme as conveniently yt may after my burial, be removed, brought and layde nye the place of my sepulture, In wch place I will my Executors to cawse to be made honorable tombs or monuments for a decent memory of us.'

Source: www.tudorhistory.org and J. M. Stone, *Mary I: Queen of England*, pp.507–20 (pub. 1901); from a transcript in the Harleian MSS (6949). The original is no longer extant.

Notes

Chapter 1 – Infanta of Spain
1. Amy Licence, *Catherine of Aragon: An Intimate Life of Henry VIII's True Wife*, p.11.
2. Giles Tremlett, *Isabella of Castile: Europe's First Great Queen*, p.282.
3. David Starkey, *Six Wives: The Queens of Henry VIII*, p.11.
4. Giles Tremlett, *Isabella of Castile: Europe's First Great Queen*, pp.17–25.
5. Ibid., pp.34–35.
6. https://web.archive.org/web/20190330183046/https://www.nationalgeographic.com/archaeology-and-history/magazine/2019/march-april/queen-isabellas-rise-to-spanish-throne/.
7. Giles Tremlett, *Isabella of Castile: Europe's First Great Queen*, p.64.
8. See note 6.
9. https://www.britannica.com/biography/Ferdinand-II-king-of-Spain.
10. https://www.britannica.com/biography/Carlos-de-Aragon-principe-de-Viana.
11. Giles Tremlett, *Isabella of Castile: Europe's First Great Queen*, p.71.
12. Ibid., pp.165–66.
13. Ibid., p.172.
14. Ibid., p.201.
15. Amy Licence, *Catherine of Aragon: An Intimate Life of Henry VIII's True Wife*, pp.35–36.
16. Ibid., p.58.
17. Ibid., pp.37–42.
18. Ibid., pp.42–44.
19. Ibid., pp.45–50.
20. Ibid., pp.50–52.

Chapter 2 – Princess of Wales
1. Calendar of State Papers Spain, Volume 1, 1485–1509. Document 13, dated 10 March 1488.
2. Calendar of State Papers Spain, Volume 1, 1485–1509. Documents 14, 15 and 16, dated 30 April 1488.
3. Gareth Streeter, *Arthur, Prince of Wales: Henrys VIII's Lost Brother*, pp.55–58.
4. Julia Fox, *Sister Queens: Katherine of Aragon and Juana Queen of Castile*, pp.26–27.
5. Ibid., pp.28–29.
6. Ibid., pp.29–31.
7. Gareth Streeter, *Arthur, Prince of Wales: Henrys VIII's Lost Brother*, p.107.
8. Calendar of State Papers Spain, Volume 1, 1485–1509. Document 249, dated 11 January 1500.
9. Gareth Streeter, *Arthur, Prince of Wales: Henrys VIII's Lost Brother*, pp.118–119.
10. Calendar of State Papers Spain, Volume 1, 1485–1509. Document 241, Marriage Ceremony, dated 19 May 1499.
11. Theresa Earenfight, *Catherine of Aragon: Infanta of Spain, Queen of England*, p.2.
12. David Starkey, *Six Wives: The Queens of Henry VIII*, p.29.
13. Giles Tremlett, *Isabella of Castile: Europe's First Great Queen*, p.417.
14. Andrea Clarke, *Tudor Monarchs Lives in Letters*, p.25.
15. Amy Licence, *Catherine of Aragon: An Intimate Life of Henry VIII's True Wife*, pp.75–77.

16. Ibid., pp.82–85.
17. Ibid., p.86–7.
18. Alison Weir, *The Six Wives of Henry VIII*, p.28.
19. Antonia Fraser, *The Six Wives of Henry VIII*, p.30.
20. Amy Licence, *Catherine of Aragon: An Intimate Life of Henry VIII's True Wife*, p.95.
21. Ibid., pp.97–105.
22. Gareth Streeter, *Arthur, Prince of Wales: Henrys VIII's Lost Brother*, pp.131–33.

Chapter 3 – Uncertain Times

1. Amy Licence, *Catherine of Aragon: An Intimate Life of Henry VIII's True Wife*, p.123.
2. Julia Fox, *Sister Queens: Katherine of Aragon and Juana Queen of Castile*, pp.67–8.
3. Amy Licence, *Catherine of Aragon: An Intimate Life of Henry VIII's True Wife*, pp.128–9.
4. Ibid., pp.129–30.
5. Gareth Streeter, *Arthur, Prince of Wales: Henrys VIII's Lost Brother*, p.162.
6. Ibid., p.165.
7. Julia Fox, *Sister Queens: Katherine of Aragon and Juana Queen of Castile*, p.87.
8. Amy Licence, *Catherine of Aragon: An Intimate Life of Henry VIII's True Wife*, pp.144–47.
9. Ibid., p.150.
10. Giles Tremlett, *Isabella of Castile: Europe's First Great Queen*, p.419.
11. Amy Licence, *Catherine of Aragon: An Intimate Life of Henry VIII's True Wife*, pp.152–3.
12. Ibid., p.154.
13. Ibid., p.162.
14. Ibid., pp.166–69.
15. Anne Crawford, *Letters of the Queens of England*, pp.167–168.
16. Calendar of State Papers Spain, Volume 1, 1485–1509. Document 484, dated 28 August 1506.
17. Amy Licence, *Catherine of Aragon: An Intimate Life of Henry VIII's True Wife*, pp.175–80.
18. https://www.hrp.org.uk/hampton-court-palace/history-and-stories/katherine-of-aragon/#gs.c7mgrt.
19. Julia Fox, *Sister Queens: Katherine of Aragon and Juana Queen of Castile*, pp.146–47.

Chapter 4 – Queen of England

1. Amy Licence, *Catherine of Aragon: An Intimate Life of Henry VIII's True Wife*, p.187.
2. David Starkey, *Henry: Virtuous Prince*, p.281.
3. Ibid., p.278.
4. Ibid., pp.288–89.
5. Amy Licence, *Catherine of Aragon: An Intimate Life of Henry VIII's True Wife*, p.201.
6. Ibid.
7. Ibid., p.203.
8. Ibid., p.204.
9. More (copyright), Yale University Press.
10. Amy Licence, *Catherine of Aragon: An Intimate Life of Henry VIII's True Wife*, p.200.
11. Anne Crawford, *Letters of the Queens of England*, pp.169–170.

Chapter 5 – Good Queen Catherine

1. David Starkey, *Henry: Virtuous Prince*, pp.306–308.
2. Julia Fox, *Sister Queens: Katherine of Aragon and Juana Queen of Castile*, p.166.
3. https://www.theguardian.com/culture/2023/jan/31/metal-detectorist-tudor-gold-pendant-henry-viii-katherine-of-aragon-warwickshire.
4. Julia Fox, *Sister Queens: Katherine of Aragon and Juana Queen of Castile*, pp.167–168.

5. https://www.bbc.co.uk/news/uk-42429199; Henry VIII spent almost an entire year's tax on a series of lavish events.
6. Amy Licence, *Catherine of Aragon: An Intimate Life of Henry VIII's True Wife*, p.215.
7. Ibid., p.230.
8. Ibid., p.234.
9. Letters and Papers, Foreign and Domestic, Henry VIII, Volume 1, 1509–1514: Letter 119 – King Henry VIII to King Ferdinand of Aragon, dated 26 July 1509.
10. See note 8.
11. Amy Licence, *Catherine of Aragon: An Intimate Life of Henry VIII's True Wife*, p.235.
12. Anne Crawford, *Letters of the Queens of England*, pp.171–172.
13. Ibid., pp.172–173.
14. Amy Licence, *Catherine of Aragon: An Intimate Life of Henry VIII's True Wife*, p.240.
15. https://www.historic-uk.com/HistoryUK/HistoryofScotland/The-Battle-of-Flodden/.
16. Andrea Clarke, *Tudor Monarchs Live in Letters*, p.61.
17. Amy Licence, *Catherine of Aragon: An Intimate Life of Henry VIII's True Wife*, p.246.
18. Ibid., p.251.
19. Letters and Papers, Foreign and Domestic, Henry VIII, Volume 2, 1515–1518: Letter 222 – Charles Brandon, Duke of Suffolk to Cardinal Thomas Wolsey, dated 5 March 1515.
20. Amy Licence, *Catherine of Aragon: An Intimate Life of Henry VIII's True Wife*, p.266–268.
21. Ibid., p.268.
22. Ibid., p.271–72.
23. Ibid., p.273.
24. Julia Fox, *Sister Queens: Katherine of Aragon and Juana Queen of Castile*, p.231.
25. David Starkey, *Six Wives: The Queens of Henry VIII*, p.187.
26. Amy Licence, *Catherine of Aragon: An Intimate Life of Henry VIII's True Wife*, pp.286–291.
27. David Starkey, *Six Wives: The Queens of Henry VIII*, pp.181–82.
28. Alison Weir, *The Six Wives of Henry VIII*, p.131.
29. https://www.hrp.org.uk/hampton-court-palace/history-and-stories/the-field-of-cloth-of-gold/#gs.c91f6v.
30. Amy Licence, *Catherine of Aragon: An Intimate Life of Henry VIII's True Wife*, p.295.
31. https://www.worldhistory.org/Diet_of_Worms/.
32. https://www.churchofengland.org/media/stories-and-features/why-king-known-defender-faith.
33. Letters and Papers, Foreign and Domestic, Henry VIII, Volume 3, 1519–1523: Letter 2848 – Adrian VI to Katharine of Arragon, dated 23 February 1523.
34. Amy Licence, *Catherine of Aragon: An Intimate Life of Henry VIII's True Wife*, pp.297–98.

Chapter 6 – Motherhood

1. Amy Licence, *In Bed with the Tudors: The Sex Lives of a Dynasty from Elizabeth of York to Elizabeth I*, p.44.
2. Ibid., p.79.
3. https://www.tudorsociety.com/catherine-of-aragons-stillbirth-on-31-january-1510-the-primary-source/?utm_content=cmp-true.
4. Ibid.
5. Julia Fox, *Sister Queens: Katherine of Aragon and Juana Queen of Castile*, pp.175–77.
6. Amy Licence, *Catherine of Aragon: An Intimate Life of Henry VIII's True Wife*, pp.224–228.
7. https://www.westminster-abbey.org/abbey-commemorations/royals/henry-son-of-henry-viii.
8. Nicholas Orme, *Tudor Children*, p.27.
9. https://www.tudorsociety.com/the-pregnancies-of-katherine-of-aragon-by-sarah-bryson/?utm_content=cmp-true.

10. Ibid.
11. Linda Porter, *Mary Tudor: The First Queen*, p.6.
12. Anna Whitelock, *Mary Tudor: England's First Queen*, p.10.
13. Linda Porter, *Mary Tudor: The First Queen*, p.13.
14. Anna Whitelock, *Mary Tudor: England's First Queen*, p.7.
15. Amy Licence, *Catherine of Aragon: An Intimate Life of Henry VIII's True Wife*, p.280.
16. Ibid., pp.280–81.
17. Julia Fox, *Sister Queens: Katherine of Aragon and Juana Queen of Castile*, p.212.

Chapter 7 – Anne Boleyn and The King's Great Matter

1. Julia Fox, *Sister Queens: Katherine of Aragon and Juana Queen of Castile*, p.217.
2. Linda Porter, *Mary Tudor: The First Queen*, pp.28–29.
3. Anne Crawford, *Letters of the Queens of England*, p.177.
4. Linda Porter, *Mary Tudor: The First Queen*, pp.25–26, 36, 39.
5. Amy Licence, *Catherine of Aragon: An Intimate Life of Henry VIII's True Wife*, pp.314–17.
6. Ibid., p.331.
7. Carol-Ann Johnston, *Jane Seymour: An Illustrated Life*, pp.23–27.
8. Ibid.
9. Amy Licence, *Catherine of Aragon: An Intimate Life of Henry VIII's True Wife*, p.340.
10. Ibid., pp.338–39.
11. https://www.theanneboleynfiles.com/anne-boleyn-and-catherine-of-aragon-part-1/#google_vignette.
12. Amy Licence, *Catherine of Aragon: An Intimate Life of Henry VIII's True Wife*, p.342.
13. Letters and Papers, Foreign and Domestic, Henry VIII, Volume 4, 1524–1530: Letter 4858 – Campeggio to Sanga, dated 17 October 1528.
14. Ibid.
15. Letters and Papers, Foreign and Domestic, Henry VIII, Volume 4, 1524–1530: Letter 4875 – Campeggio to Salviati, dated 26 October 1528.
16. Amy Licence, *Catherine of Aragon: An Intimate Life of Henry VIII's True Wife*, pp.352–53.
17. Julia Fox, *Sister Queens: Katherine of Aragon and Juana Queen of Castile*, p.294.
18. Ibid., p.295.
19. https://www.newadvent.org/cathen/03223a.htm.
20. Amy Licence, *Catherine of Aragon: An Intimate Life of Henry VIII's True Wife*, p.368.
21. Ibid., pp.268–369.
22. David Starkey, *Six Wives: The Queens of Henry VIII*, p.241.
23. George Cavendish, *Life of Cardinal Wolsey* and https://thetudortravelguide.com/2019/06/08/blackfriars/.
24. Amy Licence, *Catherine of Aragon: An Intimate Life of Henry VIII's True Wife*, p.371.
25. Ibid., pp.374–75.
26. https://www.british-history.ac.uk/letters-papers-hen8/vol4/cdlxxxviii-dxl.
27. Letters and Papers, Foreign and Domestic, Henry VIII, Volume 4, 1524–1530: Letter 5969 – The Divorce.

Chapter 8 – Exile

1. https://www.theanneboleynfiles.com/this-book-is-for-me-and-all-kings-to-read-henry-viii-tyndale-and-anne-boleyn/#google_vignette.
2. Amy Licence, *Catherine of Aragon: An Intimate Life of Henry VIII's True Wife*, pp.386–88.
3. Ibid., p.394.
4. Ibid., pp.395–396
5. Ibid., p.396.

6. Ibid., p.399.
7. https://www.theanneboleynfiles.com/catherine-aragon-tells-henry-viii-quit-evil-life/.
8. Amy Licence, *Catherine of Aragon: An Intimate Life of Henry VIII's True Wife*, pp.425–26.
9. Letters and Papers, Foreign and Domestic, Henry VIII, Volume 5, 1531–1532: Letter 361, Chapuys to Charles V, dated 31 July 1531.
10. Letters and Papers, Foreign and Domestic, Henry VIII, Volume 5, 1531–1532: Letter 416, Chapuys to Charles V, dated 10 September 1531.
11. Letters and Papers, Foreign and Domestic, Henry VIII, Volume 5, 1531–1532: Letter 478, Chapuys to Charles V, dated 16 October 1531.
12. Letters and Papers, Foreign and Domestic, Henry VIII, Volume 5, 1531–1532: Letter 513, Katherine of Arragon to Charles V, dated 6 November 1531.
13. Letters and Papers, Foreign and Domestic, Henry VIII, Volume 5, 1531–1532: Letter 1377, Chapuys to Charles V, dated 1 October 1532.
14. Ibid.
15. https://www.theanneboleynfiles.com/25-january-1533-henry-viii-finally-marries-anne-boleyn/.
16. Amy Licence, *Catherine of Aragon: An Intimate Life of Henry VIII's True Wife*, pp.452–453.
17. https://tudortimes.co.uk/daily-life/anne-boleyns-coronation/by-barge-to-the-tower-of-london.
18. Letters and Papers, Foreign and Domestic, Henry VIII, Volume 6, 1533: Letter 760, The Divorce, dated 3 July 1533.
19. Amy Licence, *Catherine of Aragon: An Intimate Life of Henry VIII's True Wife*, p.459.
20. Ibid.
21. Letters and Papers, Foreign and Domestic, Henry VIII, Volume 6, 1533: Letter 918, Chapuys to Charles V, dated 30 July 1533.
22. Ibid.
23. Letters and Papers, Foreign and Domestic, Henry VIII, Volume 7, 1534: Letter 83, Chapuys to Charles V, dated 16 January 1534.
24. https://www.newadvent.org/cathen/02319b.htm.
25. Anne Crawford, *Letters of the Queens of England*, pp.177–78.
26. Letters and Papers, Foreign and Domestic, Henry VIII, Volume 7, 1534: Letter 1013, Chapuys to Charles V, dated 27 July 1534.
27. Amy Licence, *Catherine of Aragon: An Intimate Life of Henry VIII's True Wife*, p.472.
28. Ibid., pp.473–4.

Chapter 9 – Death of the Queen

1. Letters and Papers, Foreign and Domestic, Henry VIII, Volume 8, January– July 1535: Letter 895, The Charter House Monks, dated 19 June 1535.
2. https://www.catholicculture.org/culture/library/view.cfm?id=7604.
3. https://thomasmorestudies.org/library/. See Paris Newsletter: Account of More's Trial and Execution, 1535.
4. Letters and Papers, Foreign and Domestic, Henry VIII, Volume 9, August– December 1535: Letter 588 Katharine of Arragon to Paul III, dated 10 October 1535.
5. Letters and Papers, Foreign and Domestic, Henry VIII, Volume 9, August– December 1535: Letter 964 Chapuys to Charles V, dated 13 December 1535.
6. Letters and Papers, Foreign and Domestic, Henry VIII, Volume 9, August– December 1535: Letter 1036 Chapuys to Charles V, dated 30 December 1535.
7. Letters and Papers, Foreign and Domestic, Henry VIII, Volume 9, August– December 1535: Letter 1040 Lady Mary Wyllughby to Cromwell, dated 30 December 1535.
8. Amy Licence, *Catherine of Aragon: An Intimate Life of Henry VIII's True Wife*, p.492.

9. Letters and Papers, Foreign and Domestic, Henry VIII, Volume 10, January– June 1536: Letter 59 Chapuys to Charles V, dated 9 January 1536.
10. Letters and Papers, Foreign and Domestic, Henry VIII Volume 10, January– June 1536: Letter 28- Sir Edmund Bedy[ngfield] to Cromwell, 5 January 1536.
11. Ibid.
12. Letters and Papers, Foreign and Domestic, Henry VIII, Volume 10, January– June 1536: Letter 141 Chapuys to Charles V, dated 21 January 1536.
13. Giles Tremlett, *Catherine of Aragon: Henry's Spanish Queen*, p.421.
14. Anne Crawford, *Letters of the Queens of England*, pp.179–180.

Chapter 10 – Afterlife

1. Letters and Papers, Foreign and Domestic, Henry VIII, Volume 10, January– June 1536: Letter 59 Chapuys to Charles V, dated 9 January 1536.
2. Amy Licence, *Catherine of Aragon: An Intimate Life of Henry VIII's True Wife*, p.495.
3. Letters and Papers, Foreign and Domestic, Henry VIII, Volume 10, January– June 1536: Letter 141 Chapuys to Charles V, dated 21 January 1536.
4. Amy Licence, *Catherine of Aragon: An Intimate Life of Henry VIII's True Wife*, p.498.
5. Letters and Papers, Foreign and Domestic, Henry VIII, Volume 10, January– June 1536: Letter 40 Will of Katharine of Arragon.
6. Letters and Papers, Foreign and Domestic, Henry VIII, Volume 10, January– June 1536: Letter 39 Burial of Katharine of Arragon, dated 7 January 1536.
7. Anna Whitelock, *Mary Tudor: England's First Queen*, p.77.
8. Letters and Papers, Foreign and Domestic, Henry VIII, Volume 10, January– June 1536: Letter 282 Chapuys to Charles V, dated 10 February 1536.
9. https://archive.org/details/ACatalogueOfTheManuscripts1802/page/n433/mode/2up?view=theater.
10. Anna Whitelock, *Mary Tudor: England's First Queen*, pp86–87.
11. Anne Crawford, *Letters of the Queens of England*, p.178.
12. https://www.historyextra.com/period/tudor/mary-i-bloody-facts-life-death-legacy-illiegitimate-henry-viii/.
13. Antonia Fraser, *The Six Wives of Henry VIII*, p.524.
14. https://www.peterborough-cathedral.org.uk/home/mary-queen-of-scots.aspx.
15. https://www.peterborough-cathedral.org.uk/old-scarlett.aspx.
16. https://www.stgeorges-windsor.org/wp-content/uploads/2017/08/BackgroundNotesHenryVIII.pdf.
17. The Reverend W.D. Sweeting, *The Cathedral Church of Peterborough: A description of its fabric and a brief history of the Episcopal See*. https://www.ajhw.co.uk/books/book350/book350e/book350e.html.
18. Alison Weir, *The Six Wives of Henry VIII*, p.300.
19. https://spartacus-educational.com/Katherine_Hare.htm.
20. https://www.peterborough-cathedral.org.uk/newsarticle.aspx/41/the_katharine_of_aragon_festival_2024_gets_underway.
21. Antonia Fraser, *The Six Wives of Henry VIII*, p.525.
22. Alison Weir, *The Six Wives of Henry VIII*, pp.300–301.

Bibliography

Books

Earenfight, Theresa, *Catherine of Aragon: Infanta of Spain, Queen of England,* Penn State University Press, Pennsylvania, 2022.

Fox, Julia, *Sister Queens: Katherine of Aragon and Juana Queen of Castile,* Ballantine Books, New York, 2012.

Fraser, Antonia, *The Six Wives of Henry VIII,* W&N, London, 2009.

Licence, Amy, *Catherine of Aragon: An Intimate Life of Henry VIII's True Wife,* Amberley Publishing, Gloucestershire, 2016.

Licence, Amy, *In Bed with the Tudors: The Sex Lives of a Dynasty from Elizabeth of York to Elizabeth I,* Amberley Publishing, Gloucestershire, 2012.

Orme, Nicholas, *Tudor Children,* Yale University Press, Connecticut, 2023.

Porter, Linda, *Mary Tudor: The First Queen,* Piatkus, London, 2009.

Starkey, David, *Henry: Virtuous Prince,* Harper Perennial, New York, 2009.

Starkey, David, *Six Wives: The Queens of Henry VIII,* Vintage, New York, 2004.

Streeter, Gareth, *Arthur, Prince of Wales: Henrys VIII's Lost Brother,* Pen & Sword History, Barnsley, South Yorkshire, 2023.

Tremlett, Giles, *Catherine of Aragon: Henry's Spanish Queen,* Faber & Faber, London, 2011.

Tremlett, Giles, *Isabella of Castile: Europe's First Great Queen,* Bloomsbury Paperbacks, London, 2017.

Weir, Alison, *The Six Wives of Henry VIII,* Vintage Publishing, London, 2007.

Whitelock, Anna, *Mary Tudor: England's First Queen,* Bloomsbury Publishing PLC, London, 2009.

Online Sources

Letters and Papers, Foreign and Domestic, Henry VIII
https://www.british-history.ac.uk/series/letters-and-papers-henry-viii
Calendar of State Papers, Spain, Volume 1, 1485–1509
https://www.british-history.ac.uk/cal-state-papers/spain/vol1.

Index

Abel, Thomas 125, 133
Adrian VI, Pope 80
Ainsworth, Henry 12
Alcacovas (Treaty) 7
Alcala de Henares 1–2
Alfonso V of Portugal 3
Alfonso XI of Castile 4
Alfonso, Prince of Asturias 2–3
Alhambra Palace 9, 11
Alhambra Decree 9
Almazan, Miguel Perez 45
Alvara de Alba 7
Amadas, Robert 67
Ampthill 126, 128–129
Angus, Archibald, 6th Earl of Douglas 72
Aragon 4, 12, 37–38
Athequa, Jorge de, Bishop of Llandaff 142

Baeza, Gonzalo de 5
Barton, Elizabeth (Holy Maid of Kent) 129–130
Bay of Biscay 22
Beaufort, Margaret, Countess of Richmond 17, 25, 53
Bedingfield, Sir Henry 140–141
Berengaria of Castile 95
Blackfriars (Legatine Court) 106–108, 113–114, 116
Blount, Lady Elizabeth 'Bessie' 90
Boabdil, (Abi Abdilehi) 8
Boleyn, Anne 58, 95–103, 114, 117, 119, 121, 124–130, 136, 145–150
Boleyn, Mary 97, 99
Boleyn, Thomas 78, 87, 95, 96, 119, 146
Bourchier, Henry, Earl of Essex 87
Brandon, Charles 70–71, 111, 126, 133–34, 139
Brandon, Eleanor 148
Brittany 22
Bryan, Lady Margaret 89
Buckden House 128, 133
Burgh, Sir Thomas 126–127
Burgundy 13–14, 16, 40
Butler, Sir James 96–97

Calais 13, 63, 65, 76, 78, 125, 152
Cambria, Countess of 28
Campeggio, Cardinal Lorenzo 103–106, 111–112
Canterbury 63– 64, 75, 87, 120
Carmona, Elena de 5

Carthusian Order/ Carthusian Martyrs of London 137
Cassery, Frances de 63–64
Castile 2–5, 8, 37–39, 43, 89, 95
Catherine of Lancaster 1
Catherine of Valois 17
Catherine of York, Countess of Devon 89
Cecily of York 26
Chapuys, Eustace 115, 119, 123, 125, 128, 129–132, 135, 138–143, 145, 148–150
Charles V, Emperor 44– 45, 68, 73, 75–76, 78–79, 81, 89, 94, 100–101, 106–107, 117–119, 122, 129, 132, 138, 145, 149, 165
Cheapside 48–49
Churching 84
Cisneros, Francisco Jimenez de, Bishop of Toledo 9, 44
Claude, Queen 76, 78, 96, 125
Clayton, Katharine 155
Clement VII, Pope 101, 103, 136
Clerk, John, Bishop of Bath and Wells 106–107
Columbus, Christopher 10–11
Compton, William 83
Constance of Castile 1
Coruña 22
Cranmer, Thomas Archbishop of Canterbury 126
Cromwell, Thomas 133–134, 138–140, 145, 149
Cuero, Juan de 29
Cueva, Beltran de la 2

Daubney, Giles 13
Deane, Henry Archbishop of Canterbury 25, 28
Deuteronomy 98
Deza, Fray Diego 6
Diet of Worms 79
Dimmock, Sir John 51
Dogmersfield House 23
Dover 63, 76, 81
Dudley, Edmund 55
Durham House 34, 37, 40

Edward IV 16, 18–19, 31, 98
Edward V 16–17
Eleanor of Austria 44, 125
Elizabeth of York 17–18, 21, 26, 32, 34–36, 43, 65, 71
Ely House 124
Empson, Richard 55

Index

England 1, 12–13, 16–20, 22–24, 26–27, 29, 31, 34, 36–37, 39–43, 45, 47–53, 56–57, 60, 62–63, 65–67, 69–70, 72, 74–76, 78–79, 81, 86, 88, 91, 93–101, 103–107, 110–111, 114–115, 117, 119–121, 123–126, 130, 132–133, 136–137, 140, 144, 146–148, 150–153, 155–156
English Channel 13, 22
Enrique IV (Henry) of Castile 2–3, 95
Erasmus, Desiderius 7, 80, 92
Exeter 22

Farthingale 56, 58
Federston, Master 92
Ferdinand II of Aragon 2–16, 19–22, 37–38, 40–46, 51–54, 60–61, 68–69, 80, 82–83, 88, 90, 95, 100, 109
Fernandez, Fray Diego 42, 69–70, 82–83
Field of the Cloth of Gold 76–79
Fisher, John, Bishop of Rochester 107– 108, 111, 125, 135, 137, 142
Fitzroy, Henry, Duke of Richmond and Somerset 90, 93
Flodden 66– 68, 72, 88
Forest, Bishop John 134
Foxe, Richard, Bishop of Exeter 13, 46
France 12–14, 16, 43, 60–64, 66–70, 72, 75–76, 78–79, 81, 84, 88, 94–96, 114, 120, 125–126
Francis I 70, 75–78, 81, 94, 100, 125
Fuensalida, Gutierre Gomez de 44, 46–47

Galindo, 'La Latina' Beatriz 6
George, Duke of Clarence 18–19, 31
George V 156
Geraldini, Alessandro 74
Germaine of Foix 88
Giustinian, Sebastian 71, 88–90
Granada 7–9, 21–22, 43, 51,
Greenwich 37, 46–47, 53, 58, 63, 71, 73, 81, 89, 134
Grey, Lady Jane 151–152
Grey, Sir Thomas 60–61, 87
Griffith, Master 110
Guadalupe 22
Gunthorpe, John, Dean of Wells 12

H & K Pendant 56
Hall, Edward 88
Hampton Court Palace 82
Henry, Duke of Cornwall 84– 88
Henry V 17
Henry VI 17
Henry VII 12–13, 16, 18, 21, 34–35, 38, 43, 45, 55, 60, 66, 71, 100, 109
Henry VIII 2, 7, 25, 32–40, 42, 44–53, 55–81, 83–90, 92–150, 152–153, 155, 157
Hilsey, John, Bishop of Rochester 148
Hood, Robin 59, 72
Howard, Agnes, 2nd Duchess of Norfolk 28, 89
Howard, Sir Edmund 66
Howard, Sir Edward 60

Howard, Lady Elizabeth 95
Howard, Thomas, 2nd Earl of Surrey/ Duke of Norfolk 66–68
Howard, Thomas, 3rd Duke of Norfolk 95, 120, 125–126, 149

Isabella of Aragon 4, 7, 14–16
Isabella of Castile 2–16, 19, 21–22, 36–38, 42, 51–52, 60, 80, 88, 90, 94–95, 134
Isabel of Portugal 2
Isabella of Portugal 94, 118–119

James IV of Scotland 18, 36, 66–68, 72–73
James V of Scotland 67, 72
John of Gaunt 1, 17
Juan (John) II of Aragon 4
Juan (John) II of Castile 1, 2
Juan (John) Prince of Asturias and Girona 3, 4, 5, 14–15
Juana Enriquez 4
Juana (Joanna) of Castile 4, 13, 14–16, 22, 37–40, 43–44, 52, 89–90, 94
Juana of Portugal 2
Juana (la Beltraneja) 2– 4, 7
Julius II, Pope 60

Kimbolton Castle 132–134, 138, 140–141, 143, 146
Kingston upon Thames 25

Lancaster 1, 17, 25
Lee, Edward, Archbishop of York 116, 121, 123, 134
Leon 3
Leviticus 98
Longland, John, Bishop of Lincoln 106, 121
Longueville, Duke of 65
London 25–26, 28, 34, 37, 41, 47–49, 56, 58, 84, 103–104, 112, 116, 133, 136–137, 139
Lopez, Juan 42
Louis XII 60, 62, 68, 70, 84, 96
Louise of Savoy 78
Lovell, Thomas 66
Linacre, Thomas 92
Los Ojos de Huecar 7
Ludlow Castle 21, 24, 30–31, 33, 55, 94
Luther, Martin 79–81

Maria of Aragon 4–5, 16, 90, 94, 100, 118
Maria of Hungary 119
Manuel I of Portugal 16, 90, 100
Manuel, Duenna Elvira 24, 31, 40
Marello, Cecilia 7
Margaret of Anjou 61
Margaret of Austria 14–15, 40, 78–79, 84, 95–96, 119
Margaret, Dowager Duchess of Burgundy 18
Martir, Pedro 6, 88
Mary of Teck 156
Mary, Queen of Scots 152–153

178 Catherine of Aragon

Maximilian of Austria, Emperor 14, 18, 63, 68, 75
May Day Riots 73
Medina del Campo (Treaty) 13, 20
Mendoza, Inigo de 115
Miguel de la Paz 16
More, Sir Thomas 51–52, 80, 92, 135, 138
More (The) 122–123
Mountjoy, Lord William 65, 126–127
Musettula, John Antony 112–113
Muxica, Martin de 61

Nebrija, Antonia de 7
Neville, Queen Anne 47
Neville, Isabel, Duchess of Clarence 19

Pageants 7, 25, 28, 29, 52–53, 59, 86, 97
Palencias, Alonso de 7
Paul III, Pope 136–137
Percy, Henry, Earl of Northumberland 97
Peterborough Cathedral 147–148, 152–154, 156
Philip of Burgundy 13–14, 38–40, 43
Plantagenet, Edward, 17th Earl of Warwick 18–20, 31
Plymouth 22
Pole, Cardinal Reginald 19
Pole, Edmund de la 40
Pole, Margaret 19, 31, 55–56, 89
Pole, Richard 31
Pomegranate 51, 55–57, 86, 148, 156
Poison 4, 129, 145–146
Portugal 1, 7, 16, 90
Puebla, Rodrigo Gonzalez de la 12–13, 20, 29–31, 37, 40, 44, 105

Richard III 16–19, 31, 47
Richard, Duke of York 16–17
Richmond 17, 37, 41, 42, 45, 59, 63–64, 66, 84, 86–87, 90, 93,117, 122

Sa, John de la 139
Salinas (Willoughby), Maria de 69, 140–141, 148, 155
Salisbury House 37
Santander 15
Sansovino, Jacopo 153
Santa Maria de la Sede 7
Santiago de Compostela 22
Savage, Thomas, Doctor of Law 12
Scarlett, (Old) Robert 153
Scotland 18, 36, 66–67, 72–73, 153
Seymour, Jane 56, 149–150
Siculus, Lucio Marineo 6
Somersham Palace 133
Spain 1–2, 7, 9–13, 15, 20, 26–27, 29, 31, 33, 36–37, 40–43, 45, 50, 60, 68, 74–75, 79, 84, 86, 88, 100, 103, 105–106, 109–111, 115–116, 129, 134, 148, 156
Spanish Chronicle 100
Spanish Inquisition 9–10
St Paul's Cathedral 25–26, 29,

Stafford, Edward, Duke of Buckingham 25, 48, 51, 83
Stafford, Henry, Earl of Wiltshire 87
Stewart, John, Duke of Albany 72
Swynford, Kathryn 17

Talavera, Fernando de, Bishop of Granada 9
Thomas, William 47
Tickenhill Manor 20
Toleda 22
Torquemada, Tomas de 10
Torrigiano, Pietro 153
Tower of London 16–19, 36, 48, 65, 84, 123, 125, 133, 135, 149
Treaty of Granada 8–9
Tudor, Elizabeth, Princess (later Queen Elizabeth I) 93, 129–130, 146, 152–153
Tudor, Prince Arthur 12–13, 16, 19–21, 24–34, 36, 40, 74, 94, 98–99, 103–106, 111, 113, 115, 120, 121–122, 126–127, 135, 143
Tudor, Edmund, Duke of Richmond 17
Tudor, Prince Edward 84, 150–151
Tudor, Margaret, Queen of Scotland 34–35, 66, 72–73
Tudor, Mary (Catherine's daughter and later Queen Mary I) 26, 81, 89–95, 122, 130, 140, 143–144, 146, 149–152
Tudor, Mary (The French Queen and Catherine's sister-in-law) 35, 37, 42–45, 68–71, 76, 78, 126
Tunstall, Cuthbert, Bishop of Durham 134
Tyndale, William 114

Urswik, Christopher, Great Almoner 12

Val d'Or (the Golden Valley) 77
Valladolid 22, 42
Vere, John de, Earl of Oxford 28–29
Vergara, Isabel de 7
Vives, Juan Luis 91–92

Wales 13, 19–21, 30–33, 41–42, 63, 93, 100
Warbeck, Perkin 18–19
Warham, William, Archbishop of Canterbury 47, 84, 126
Wars of the Roses 13, 17
Westminster Abbey 27, 49–50, 87, 152–153
Westminster Palace 36–37, 49, 51, 73, 84–86
Weston, John, Prior St John of Jerusalem in England 12
Windsor 37, 40, 81, 119, 121–122
Wolsey, Cardinal Thomas 63–65, 70, 73, 76, 78, 80–81, 89, 98, 101–103, 105–106, 111, 116–117, 133
Woodstock Palace 20, 121
Woodville, Queen Elizabeth 16–18, 98
Worcester Cathedral 33
Wriothesley, Charles 149

York 16–17, 25–26, 33–36, 43, 71, 116, 134

Zamora 22